twilight
garden

First published in the United Kingdom in 2011 by
Pavilion Books
10 Southcombe Street
London W14 0RA

An imprint of Anova Books Company Ltd

Text © Lia Leendertz
Design and layout © Pavilion Books
Photography © see picture credits on page 207
Illustrations © Karolin Schnoor

Commissioning Editor: Emily Preece-Morrison
Cover Design and concept: Georgina Hewitt
Layout: Louise Leffler
Picture Research: Jenny Faithfull
Editors: Hilary Mandleberg, Nicola Hodgson
Illustrations: Karolin Schnoor
Indexer: Sandra Shotter

ISBN: 9781862059115

A CIP catalogue record for this book is available from the British Library.

Reproduction by Mission productions, Hong Kong.
Printed and bound by 1010 Printing International, China.

www.anovabooks.com

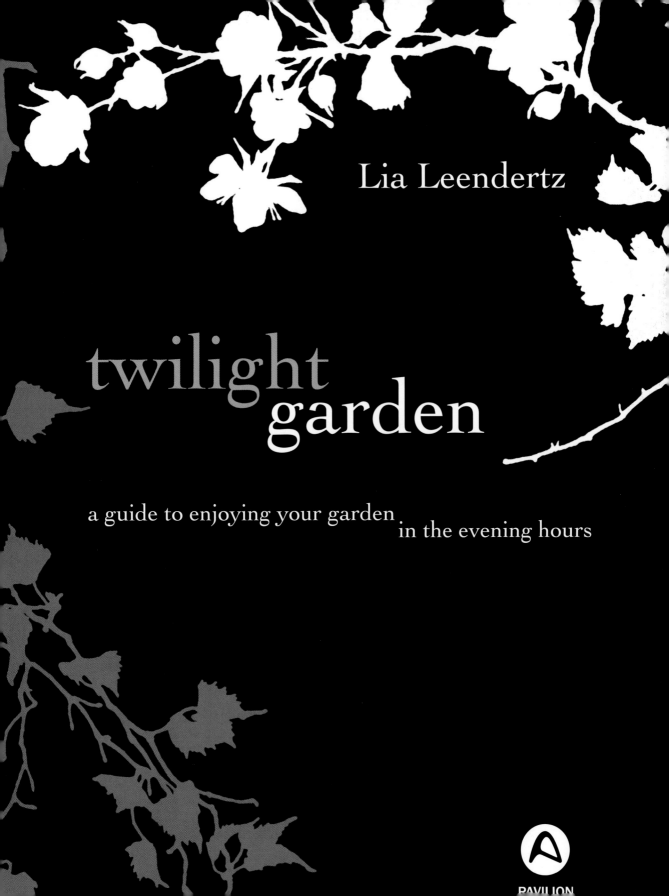

Lia Leendertz

twilight
garden

a guide to enjoying your garden in the evening hours

PAVILION

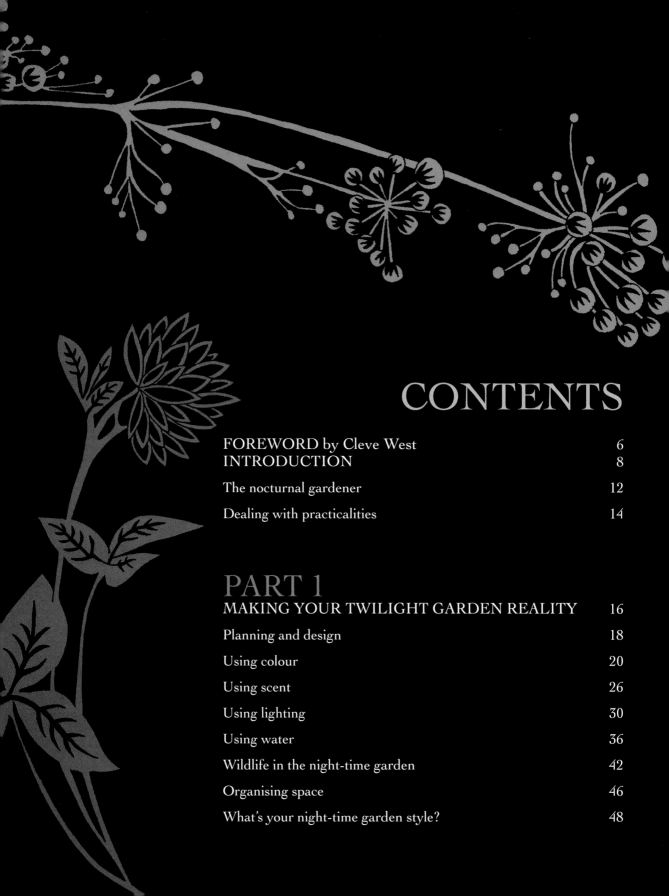

CONTENTS

FOREWORD

People love gardens. Even people without a horticultural bone in their body can appreciate the pleasure of taking fresh air in pleasant surroundings. For those of us who are hooked (and there are millions of us around the world), our own gardens exist as private sanctuaries. Ever since the concept of paradise emerged from Persia some 3,000 years ago, gardens have served as an escape from work, domestic routine and the harsh realities of life. But with the increasing pace of modern living, many of us are left wanting when it comes to actually enjoying the fruits of our labour. Long office hours leave little time, if any, to enjoy the garden in daylight, and flurries of activity over weekends to 'catch up' can leave us exhausted and frustrated. But the garden doesn't just disappear at sunset. As the background din surrenders to the last snatches of birdsong, a palpable change takes place, as emphasis shifts and our senses tune in to a different dimension. Moods and feelings that are absent by day invite you to draw breath and take a draught of twilight before the garden is cloaked in darkness.

Some say that these fleeting moments are the best time to enjoy a garden; a time when the spirit of the place really comes alive. As light fades, our senses sharpen. Changes in temperature and humidity capture scent, while less discernible night sounds are more prominent. Flowers and plants robbed of sunlight fade to grey tones and shadows, while whites, greys and silvers come into their own with a ghostly effect on the space they occupy. Blues too take on an electric luminosity, reflecting ultraviolet rays back into a visible spectrum as our eyes adjust to the twilight world, taking our appreciation of the garden to a new level. The night sky offers much at which to marvel; voids and masses take on uncertain form; the movements and calls of nocturnal wildlife are less familiar. It is an alien world and therefore captivating, as if we are getting to know the garden's innermost secrets.

In this book, Lia Leendertz has tried to further the appreciation of the moonlight garden. She looks at the basic design principles of what makes a twilight garden work; which elements can be exploited when day turns to night; which plants should be used and how to use them; and how to enjoy your garden best at this time. All these essential aspects are covered in order to shed a little twilight on how you might transform your own private space into a moonlit paradise.

Cleve West

Right: The White
Garden at Sissinghurst,
Kent, England, is the
ultimate model for an
evening garden.

INTRODUCTION

After dark, your garden could be a magical place. Imagine the possibilities. It could be a secret hideaway, a place to relax on your own with your senses fully attuned as you smell the sultry fragrances of night-blooming flowers and listen to the scuttling of nocturnal creatures and the trickle of water. Or you might prefer it as a venue for throwing memorable, candlelit parties warmed by wafts of gentle breezes, with the only decoration needed being the pale blooms of borders filled with plants chosen for their ability to glow in low light. Or maybe you'd like your garden to be a softly lit outdoor dining room, where the fresh air acts as a digestif, sharpening the appetite and making all the food taste delicious.

My own garden in the evening is a place of refuge. Throughout the day, it is filled with activity and brightly coloured plastic children's toys. It rings to the sound of laughter and tears and demands for drinks and snacks. But as dusk falls and children are ushered into baths and pyjamas, it becomes quiet, calm – mine.

'A Room of One's Own' is a luxury I have always envied: the garden is a place where I can simply be a creative being, free of the daily grind and the constant nurturing that comes from being a parent of young (or, I imagine, any) children. With four people in a three-bedroom house, a whole room all to myself filled with books and with a comfy old armchair and the warmth of a log-burning stove is always going to be a fantasy. But I do have my after-dark garden. This is where I get to stretch my wings and be myself, so I want it to be exciting and welcoming when I am free to spend some time in it.

This is my reason for wanting to make my garden as special as possible in the twilight hours, but there are many others. Lots of people don't even see their gardens in the daytime. It's easy to live an entirely indoor life. If you work the nine to five away from home, chances are you feel pretty removed from the outside world and from your garden in particular. You may not even have planted much in it, thinking that you're going to miss the show anyway; if all the best stuff is going to happen while you are stuck at your desk eating your sandwiches in the next town, then why should you bother?

Even if you work from home or are at home as a full-time parent, the garden just serves as a slightly worrying background during a busy day. If it does come to mind, it might simply be as another chore to be ticked off the list. Ironing? Check. Washing up? Check. Mowing the lawn? Check.

By making it into a garden that comes into its own at night, you give yourself a reason to care about it. Garden chores can then become part of the enjoyment you get from your garden, just as you get to enjoy simply being in it, pottering, looking, exploring and smelling.

If you already like to entertain and you're used to tidying away the drying-up after dinner parties or rolling back the lounge carpet for dancing, it makes sense to turn your garden into the venue. Like having friends round for drinks and meals? Imagine how much you would enjoy entertaining them in a garden that glows at night. Moving a party of any scale out of doors makes it a special event, taking it out of the everyday and into a slightly otherworldly zone. Comfy indoor seats and electric lighting are convenient, yes, but just like going camping and having picnics, the slight lack of comfort involved in eating and partying outdoors adds to the camaraderie and atmosphere.

What's more, you put your rose-tinted spectacles on when you remember outdoor events. You'll recall a night perched drunkenly on a garden wall by the light of a sputtering candle in a jar far more fondly than that other night spent comfortably snuggled into your friend's new sofa, no matter how atmospherically uplit her sitting room may have been. And if you're lucky enough to get a warm, sultry evening, there's nothing to beat the fun of eating a meal out of doors. The lighting is flattering, the food always tastes wonderful in the fresh air, and the voices and laughter are lifted and carried away across the neighbourhood on gentle breezes.

Relaxing and enjoying the twilight garden isn't only for crowds, though. You may just be someone who needs a little time alone. In that case, a few candles, your favourite drink and a rocking chair set within a pretty scented garden are all you need to make for some really special 'me' time. It's far more rewarding for the soul and better for the mood than an evening in front of the TV.

However you spend your evening time in the garden, whether it's gardening, kicking back, with friends or entirely alone, it can make you feel that you are grabbing the moment, experiencing something special, and really living life. No matter how chilly or wind-blown you get, you feel slightly more alive at the end of an evening out of doors, so it really pays to make your garden into a place where you want to be when darkness falls.

Lia Leendertz

THE NOCTURNAL GARDENER

It is easy to imagine that the daylight hours are the best time to be in the garden, and to shut the door on the whole place as soon as night starts to fall, but a garden is special in half-light and even more special in moonlight or candlelight. While some plants recede into darkness, others leap out of the gloaming. Purples and blues that can be gloomy in the day become pinpricks of vibrant colour, while white – which in the middle of a sunny day can be blinding – just glows, gently, at dusk.

Night gardening is necessarily a sensuous experience: as you rely less on sight, the other senses come into play. Many scents actually become stronger at night, and we are perhaps more likely to notice them because our sense of sight has become blunted. In addition, the sound of trickling or splashing water travels further in the still of the night, as do the sounds of any visitors to your garden.

These visitors include wildlife. If you can be still and quiet, you may find yourself surrounded by the snufflings of hedgehogs and the flutterings of moths. If you are really lucky, you might spot a bat swooping by or hear owls and foxes going about their business.

But it isn't just a question of luck. There is much you can do to make your garden more attractive to night-time wildlife; for example, by having plants that are attractive to night-flying insects and through sensitive, organic garden management.

All these things can make your garden a more exciting place to spend time in at night. If you really get it right, you might even get a glow-worm or two to light up the end of your garden.

In this book, I explore all the different aspects involved in creating a night-time garden – from how to plan your garden around your personal needs, to the mood you are trying to create, the colours to use, the best ways to attract wildlife and, finally, how to put all of those aspects together to make your garden a place you are drawn to evening after evening.

DEALING WITH THE PRACTICALITIES

Having decided how you want to use your garden and what features you are going to include, you are ready to make a start on the practicalities. Few of us have the good fortune to start with a blank canvas, so the first step is to look at the plants and hard landscaping features that are already in your garden and think about what you want to keep and what you really can't live with. It is always simpler to work around existing features.

Put particular thought into keeping as many of the existing larger plants as possible. Ripping everything out and starting again may be satisfying, but you will lose any sense of maturity in the garden and you will also create more work for yourself. Sometimes just clearing away around an old tree or shrub or doing a little judicious pruning can bring out a wonderful shape and character that you never knew it had before, so examine each plant for possibilities.

The next step is to measure out the available space and make a scale plan of your garden on graph paper. Include all of the garden's features that you intend to keep and mark the aspect on the plan – whether the garden is north-facing, west-facing, and so forth – as this will affect your choice of plants. Next, add in the new features you want to include. Cut out paper versions of them to scale and play around with them on the plan until you come up with something you're happy with.

Now you are finally ready to put any new hard landscaping in place – paths, patios, pergolas and arbours. There are many night-scented climbing plants to choose from, so try to include as many structures for them to clamber over as you possibly can.

Finally, after any major landscaping has been carried out, comes the new planting. Again, you may want to make a plan on paper before you start planting. As a quick rule of thumb, put any structural planting in first – hedges, topiary, trees and shrubs – and then 'fill in' with the other, more ephemeral, plants.

You will be keen to get on with creating your garden, whatever the time of year, but there are certain jobs that really should be done at particular times for the best results. That structural planting is really an autumn and winter job. These plants need masses of soil preparation and to get their roots into the soil during cool and wet times of the year. More ephemeral planting can be done at other times of the year, but you will find yourself doing a huge amount of watering if you plant at the height of summer, so try to avoid this.

PART 1
MAKING
YOUR
TWILIGHT
GARDEN
REALITY

PLANNING AND DESIGN

The planting, of course, is the exciting part of any garden. It is really the main ingredient of a beautiful twilight garden, although it isn't the only one. Before you put in a single plant, take some time to think through the way you are going to use your garden and how much time you actually have to garden – each type of garden has different needs in terms of hard landscaping, lighting, storage and even planting.

So, is yours a front garden or a back garden? Is it going to be a family garden or a party garden? Is it going to be a calm, relaxing, solitary space where you can go to unwind at the end of the day?

If you are planning on a family garden, you might want to include a lawn, a sandpit or other play equipment, a washing line, and some storage to put the children's toys away at the end of the day. If you think you're going to use your garden for parties, you'll need a decent-sized deck or patio. If you're more of a gourmand, then it might make sense to invest in a good, solid table and chairs, and to make your table setting the focus of the garden. If you are planning on spending quiet time alone in the garden, you might want to think about comfortable seating and some large, screening plants to make you feel tucked away and private.

Another consideration is whether you want to spend lots of time pottering and tending your plants or whether a low-maintenance garden, filled with shrubs and other plants that require little care once they are established, would suit you and your lifestyle better.

using colour

Right: Pale-coloured flowers and silvery foliage, such as that of Nepeta 'Six Hills Giant', will reflect low light.

As day turns to night, so the colours in your garden change. The bright reds, oranges and yellows that are most likely to catch your attention during the day slowly dull and deaden as the light fails. In their place comes – predominantly – white.

All the finest moonlit evening gardens are filled with white, silver and palest yellow plants. This is common sense: dark colours absorb light rather than reflect it. White, on the other hand, fires back at us every scrap of available light, so the white appears brighter as other colours fade. It is not only gardeners who have noticed this. White flowers are often pollinated by night-flying insects such as moths. These insects use the flowers' night-time glow as well as their scent to help them navigate towards them.

Silver-leaved plants are also effective reflectors of low light. The silvery effect is created by the hundreds of thousands of tiny pale hairs that cover the leaves. These plants generally thrive in full sunlight and hail from hot, Mediterranean climates. Their reflective surfaces have evolved in an attempt to fend off the worst heat of the sun and to help keep the plants cool. These reflective properties work just as well in low light or moonlight, of course, although silver-leaved plants are generally not quite as reflective as white flowers, despite their metallic element.

White leaps out of the gloom and moonlight brings it even more strongly to the foreground. That is why a twilight or evening gardener should consider white their most useful colour and should try to pack in as much of it as possible.

On the other hand, you also need to consider how much you use the garden during the day. Lots of white can be overpowering on a bright sunny day; if your garden includes a mass of white, come midsummer you'll find yourself regularly dazzled. Therefore, if you need your garden to work well in the daytime in the heat, too, it is probably best to use white a little more sparingly. Mix it in among other colours or concentrate on white-flowered climbers used at the back of borders containing other colours. If you garden in a damp climate, though, you may find that the midday-white problem isn't such a big issue. In the dull light of an overcast or rainy day, white can impart the same magical properties as it does in the evening.

OTHER COLOURS

Left Tulips 'Mount Tacoma', 'Blizzard' and 'White Parrot' in a white border.

White isn't the only colour that you should consider for your evening garden. Blues and purples, particularly the paler versions of these colours, also tend to leap out of the gloom. Not all blue or purple flowers work, but some, like those of *Verbena bonariensis* (see pp. 172–173), seem to have a second life come nightfall. These flowers are perfectly lovely in the day as they bob away on their thin, wiry little stems above the other plants in my borders, but come dusk, it is as if a tiny little light switches on inside each one, and they glow through the twilight.

Even if you do use your garden mainly at night, you won't want a garden entirely full of white flowers and silver-leaved plants; you might want to make just a few concessions to daytime viewing. It's not for me to advise on your choice of colour scheme. I don't know if you prefer hot, spicy reds and oranges; cool purples and blues; or even a hotchpotch of all the colours of the rainbow.

But what you may want to bear in mind, though, is that white shows up best against a dark background, and that background can often best be provided by foliage. So, mix plenty of foliage plants in with your whites and consider backing your evening borders with a dense, deep green hedge. Yew is the densest and darkest of greens, and will throw whites forward, but box works well, too. Used as a backdrop, even a privet hedge will serve this purpose well. What you might think of as unattractive in the daytime may not seem so offensive in the twilight.

Overleaf Mix purples, blues and pinks (here echinaceas and echinops) with paler colours, grasses and seed heads to catch evening light.

using scent

Planting for a night-time garden is really worthwhile since so many of the plants that look good at night also have delicious night-time fragrances. And one of the attractions of scent is that it's a strong trigger to memory; you may find yourself sitting in your twilight garden remembering your grandparents' honeysuckle-festooned tree or a jasmine-scented holiday evening.

The fragrance of jasmine, evening primrose, lilies and many other night-blooming plants moves up a gear as evening falls. This is all down to those night-time pollinators again (see p. 20). Of course, many flowers that are pollinated by day-flying insects also smell, but in their case, the scent is an added bonus. These flowers rely, primarily, on their looks to make themselves attractive to pollinators. Day-flying insects such as bees and butterflies have keen vision, and it is through sight that they find their sources of nectar. However, night-flying pollinators such as moths and bats have poor vision and low light to contend with, so they depend strongly on their sense of smell. It is usually the fruity or musky scent of the sturdier night-blooming plants that attracts bats, while moths pollinate the smaller, more delicate blooms that have a strong, sweet scent.

Some flowers look good by day or night, but there are others that close during the day and save up all their goodies for nightfall. These plants, such as white campion (*Silene alba*) and night-scented stock (*Matthiola bicornis*), respond to changes in light levels and temperature. They pump certain cells full of water and deflate others to allow their petals to unfurl and emit their scent at nightfall. Come dawn, the opposite occurs, and they seal themselves up firmly again to ride the day out.

POSITIONING SCENTED PLANTS

There aren't many rules governing the use of scented plants in the garden. Probably, though, you will want to surround your evening seating area with pots of scented plants so you are guaranteed a big hit of fragrance just where you want it most. Lilies, dianthus and brugmansias are among the plants that will grow well in containers, so use these and, if necessary, move them close to wherever you sit and drink your glass of wine in the evenings.

If you have a pergola near your house, you could drape it with jasmine (see pp. 96–97) to make a highly scented evening sitting area.

Bear in mind, however, that jasmine has a particularly strong smell, so be absolutely sure that you love it before planting. I think the scent is intoxicating, but some people find it unpleasantly overpowering.

Your scented plants don't always have to be right up close, however, so don't neglect to put some in the further reaches of the garden. The scents from more distant climbing roses and honeysuckle will drift across the garden and may even be more enjoyable for being slightly elusive. The best bet is to look for opportunities to fit scented plants in everywhere, planting scented shrubs in borders, scented perennials in pots, and scented climbers over walls, trellises and pergolas. Pack in as many as you can, throughout your garden, and you'll then get 'hits' of different delicious scents from various points or as you wander around the garden.

Above An enclosed space with scented plants, moving water and gentle lighting makes the perfect evening garden.

Overleaf Concentrate the planting of your scented plants along the edges of paths and close to seating areas to enjoy their fragrance.

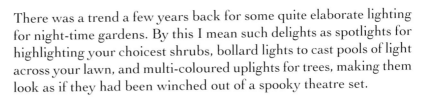

using lighting

Left Little tea lights, here held in hanging jars, cast a soft, atmospheric glow.

There was a trend a few years back for some quite elaborate lighting for night-time gardens. By this I mean such delights as spotlights for highlighting your choicest shrubs, bollard lights to cast pools of light across your lawn, and multi-coloured uplights for trees, making them look as if they had been winched out of a spooky theatre set.

For all I know, this sort of lighting may still be de rigueur in some parts of the world, but I've always felt that this approach misses some fundamental points. For one thing, these contraptions are exceedingly tricky to set up. You will need to employ an electrician, make lighting plans and dig trenches for the wires. But it is not the practicalities that really put me off; it's the effect they create – too much light, by far, and the wrong sort of light.

Night gardens should be about mystery and intrigue, and having too much in the way of electric lighting makes all intrigue go out of the window. Ever felt romantic under strip lighting? I rest my case. I appreciate that lighting effects such as these are far subtler than the movement-sensor burglar lights that dazzle the entire garden at the twitching of a cat's whiskers, but I still think they are out of place. How can you appreciate the ghostly outline of a lily in the moonlight if the tree it is next to is bathed in a vivid green glow?

CANDLELIGHT AND FAIRY LIGHTS

But a little lighting is sometimes called for. For my money, you have two wonderful options: candlelight and fairy lights. On an intimate scale, candlelight works well because it's so flattering. Eyes sparkle and skin glows. It's hard not to feel attractive when your face is lit by nothing more than gentle candlelight.

Another plus is that candlelight is easily managed; although, as with everything, there are cheap and expensive ways to go about it. Even on the stillest, warmest night there is usually enough breeze to blow a bare, unprotected candle out or to make it flicker most annoyingly. The answer could be a storm lamp. These are, essentially, large glass vases into which you place the candle. It is then completely protected from any wind, or indeed storm. However, a storm lantern is a big, expensive item, and if you're on a budget, a large glass jar will do the trick just as well. (One of the beauties of night gardening is that no-one can really see how posh your candle holder is anyway.) On a smaller scale, glass baby-food jars make the perfect holders for nightlights; if you're at the stage in your life when you have access to baby-food jars, you are likely to have lots and lots of them. I once saw nightlights used in this way at a country wedding: a couple of hundred were spaced along the top of a fence overlooking a field with hills in the background. It was magical as night fell, and I can't imagine that a more beautiful effect could have been created with a lighting budget of thousands.

If you feel you need a little more light than candle flames alone can provide, you should consider fairy lights. These are the closest that electric lighting gets to casting the magical glow you get from candlelight. And fairy lights have the added bonus that they instantly create a festive, party atmosphere, should that be what you require. I love simple ropes of fairy lights wrapped around pergolas, banisters or railings. They also look pretty draped over shrubs, although this look is more than a little reminiscent of the decorations that spring up in front gardens during the last few weeks in December. In short, they will make your shrubs look like outdoor Christmas trees, which may not be the sort of festive look you want all year round.

SOLAR-POWERED LIGHTS

With people everywhere becoming more eco-aware, there is now a wide range of solar-powered lighting on the market. You can buy solar-powered fairy lights, uplighters and indeed almost any type of gardening light you can think of.

The set-up for solar-powered lighting is much easier than for mains lighting; you don't need to worry about connecting to the mains or about installing an outdoor power point. Lights are supplied with a small, adjustable solar panel that must be positioned so that it is facing south. The panel must be outdoors (rather than, say, behind a large window) and shadows shouldn't fall on it, particularly at the prime charging time, which is between 10am and 2pm each day. The panel is adjustable so it can be angled for maximum sunlight at different times of year. In summer, when the sun is overhead, the panel will be almost flat to the ground; in autumn and spring it should be tilted up slightly; and in winter the panel must be more vertical in order to catch the sun's low rays.

Solar-powered lights can work all year round, although, obviously, they will receive a greater charge in the summer.

ELECTRIC-LIGHTING EFFECTS

Although, as I have already said, I don't particularly like electric lighting in the garden and don't choose to have it in mine, it is not my place to tell you that you shouldn't have it in yours. You can create a number of effects with electric lighting. One of these is to use spotlights to accent a particular shrub or feature, such as a large urn in a border.

'Grazing' is another effect. This is useful if you want to make a feature of a textured wall or other surface. The light fitting is positioned close to the wall so that the beam of light 'grazes' its surface, picking out any slightly raised areas and throwing tiny recesses into deep shadow.

'Moonlighting' is an effect that involves positioning soft lights in the branches of trees to recreate the effect of moonlight and to cast soft, dappled shadows.

'Shadowing' and 'silhouetting' are two sides of the same coin. 'Shadowing' involves lighting a particularly architectural plant from the front in order to cast a shadow on a wall behind. 'Silhouetting' involves lighting a similar plant from behind to create a strong silhouette when viewed from the front.

'Uplighting' is an effect that works best on well-shaped trees or groups of trees, or on statues, particularly where the statue is wider at the top than at its base.

Before going to the not-inconsiderable trouble and expense of having electric lighting installed to create effects like these, you might first want to experiment. Use a couple of high-powered torches, a camera (to record the results) and some amenable friends who don't mind standing in your shrubbery in the dark to offer their opinion.

Installing electric lighting in the garden is not a DIY job. Gardens are often wet places, and electricity and water don't mix. You must employ a qualified electrician who should ensure that the correct cables are used and that every device is connected to a residual current device (RCD), which will automatically cut off the power in the event of an accident.

using water

Left A small, still pool will reflect the moon, and even – on particularly clear nights – the stars.

A pond may not be the first thing you think of as a night-time feature, but it's wonderful for attracting wildlife, from the small and easily overlooked pond skaters and pond beetles to the more glamorous dragonflies, newts and frogs, and night-time wildlife-spotting is one of the most exciting aspects of the evening garden. If it's wildlife you're after, your pond shouldn't contain any fish, since fish will prey on the other creatures in the water. And the pond should have one shallow, beach-like edge where creatures can easily enter and exit the water. Your pond will need planting up with oxygenating plants such as *Elodea crispa* and hair grass; deep-water aquatics such as waterlilies; and marginals such as as *Lobelia fulgens*, calla and irises. With those in place, the water will remain healthy and the pond can sustain the maximum amount of wildlife.

Another night-time water feature to consider is a 'moon-gazing pond'. You can create one of these by positioning a small, still pool with a dark lining somewhere fairly open so that the pool will reflect the moon unimpeded. Be warned, though, that if your moon-gazing pond doesn't contain any plants, the water will need changing frequently or it will quickly turn stagnant.

Moving water brings a garden to life whatever the time of day. In the daylight hours, a water feature looks beautiful and provides lively, sparkling movement, but at night, when the sense of sight is dulled and the other senses are more highly attuned, the sound of a water feature is particularly appealing. A small fountain trickling away in the darkness creates a wonderful atmosphere and helps, subtly, to mask any noises coming from outside the garden. It also creates an 'off-stage' sound effect that will draw you down to the unseen parts of the garden.

Right: Underwater
lights illuminate a
hidden world and
allow a glimpse
into otherwise
murky depths.

A small wall fountain trickling into a basin of water makes a particularly lovely feature for a terrace or deck where you might sit during the evening. For an extremely effective look, build underwater lights into the basin that will light up the whole thing from below or, for a similar and, I think, equally magical effect, place a handful of floating candles on the surface of the water instead.

Just as there is solar-powered lighting, so there are solar-powered pumps and fountains that will reduce the cost and fuss of installation. These are generally designed for smaller water features, however. If you want a larger feature, such as a stream, you may have to use mains electricity to power your pump. As when installing electric lighting in the garden, you must be extremely careful with any electricity that is needed to power a pump. Always call in an electrician to ensure that all the wiring is correctly routed and all devices are correctly installed.

Overleaf Fibre-optic
underwater lights
are effective,
although a similarly
magical effect to
this beautifully lit
lily pond could be
created using
floating candles.

wildlife in the night-time garden

It's more than a little exciting to find yourself sharing your evening peace and quiet with the snuffling of a hedgehog. There are lots of animals and insects that mainly come out at night, and you will make your garden a more interesting place to be at night if you learn how to encourage them in and cater for them.

HEDGEHOGS

Hedgehogs are common in urban and suburban areas, where they find plenty of food to their liking, and plenty of good nesting spots. They can travel over large areas in search of food and they are surprisingly good climbers, so you needn't worry that they may not gain access to your well-fenced garden.

You can buy a specially made hedgehog home, which will provide a temporary nest for a few days in summer (hedgehogs tend to move around quite a lot when the going is good) or a hibernation den in winter. But you can equally well make your own. I have built one in a quiet corner of the garden using a couple of old bricks topped with a roofing tile and stuffed with leaves, twigs and straw. It has yet to lure a prickly visitor in, but it's dry and cosy. Alternatively, you could just leave piles of twigs and leaves in the garden for the hedgehogs to make their own nests. In fact, any garden that is not too tidily managed is likely to prove attractive.

Hedgehogs eat slugs, snails, caterpillars and earthworms, so the best thing you can do to encourage them is to manage your garden organically. That way, you'll have plenty of food for the hedgehogs to devour. Avoid using slug pellets, since hedgehogs may be poisoned by eating slugs that have eaten the pellets. If you want to encourage hedgehogs with food, put some tinned pet food, raw or cooked meat, muesli or chopped peanuts out as evening falls. If any food is left uneaten, bring it back in first thing in the morning. Don't put out milk and bread, as these can give hedgehogs diarrhoea.

MOTHS

Moths are the poor relative of the butterflies that flitter around our gardens during the day and delight us with their colourful, fluttering wings. Moths are far less showy and – crucially – browner and more hairy. If you can cope with the hairiness (you don't have to touch them, after all) and get a proper look at their markings, you will find that they are really quite beautiful, just in a slightly less obvious way than butterflies.

Attracting moths is mainly a matter of planting the pale-flowered night-scented plants that you're going to fill your garden with anyway. Those that are particularly good sources of nectar for moths are nicotiana (see pp. 108–109), evening primrose (see pp. 110–111), honeysuckle (see pp. 102–103) and sweet rocket (see pp. 92–93). Moths also benefit from having an area of grass left to grow long enough so that it flowers, as well as from plantings of native trees and hedges that their caterpillars can feed on.

Perhaps one of the reasons we fail to appreciate the beauty of moths is that, since they choose to come out after dark, we rarely see them. This can be remedied by setting up a moth trap. Hang a white sheet on the washing line or elsewhere in the garden and leave a bright torch shining on it. Within minutes it should be covered in moths.

You can try to identify the moths (you can buy an identification guide to help you) as they flit about, but you might find identification easier if you catch them in glass jars. Take great care not to damage the moths when you do this, and release them as soon as you can. Children love being involved in this activity, and it's a great way to lure them out into the garden of an evening.

BATS

Swooping in at nightfall, bats are an incredibly exciting addition to night-time wildlife-spotting. Many bats are now endangered due to a loss of suitable places for roosting and a lack of suitable food. This state of affairs has partly been caused by intensive farming practices, but by managing your garden organically, there is a chance that you will get the occasional bat visitor. They feed on insects, so they like gardens that are teeming with them. And if you have planted your garden up with night-blooming plants to attract night-flying insects, so much the better.

As well as planting the night-blooming and night-scented flowers listed in detail later in this book (see pp. 76–203), try planting native wildflowers and simple cottage-garden perennials. Both of these do a better job of attracting plenty of insects to your garden than highly bred bedding plants and double-flowered varieties.

Surprising though it may seem, another bat-attracting feature is a log pile. This is great for providing a home for the insects that bats feed on. Constructing a log pile is as easy as it sounds: you just need to gather a few logs and pile them up. The key then is to leave them to rot down; the more rotted they become, the more useful they are to insects. Choose a quiet corner of the garden where the logs are unlikely to be disturbed and, if possible, site the pile in shade where it won't get heated up and dried out by the sun.

If you have a suitably quiet, undisturbed spot, you might also consider putting up bat boxes. These look like bird boxes except they're entered from below, so there's a hole where there would otherwise be a floor. Bat boxes need to be on the north side of a tree or building so the sun doesn't shine directly on them during the day, which is when the bats use them. It can take a long time for bats to find bat boxes, so be patient and don't take yours down just because you don't get any residents for a couple of years.

GLOW-WORMS

Imagine sitting outside your back door and watching the soft, green glow of glow-worms providing tiny pinpoints of pale green light around your garden. They make the perfect finishing touch for a twilight garden.

Glow-worms aren't, in fact, worms at all but a kind of beetle. It is the females that glow to attract a mate. They are extremely rare, and in truth you are fairly unlikely to be able to lure them onto your patch, but by having a go, you will also be creating a garden that other forms of wildlife will love, even if you don't attract glow-worms themselves.

Glow-worms like some grass left long, but they also like to have an open area to display themselves. To ensure that they will be seen, they only start to glow when it's really dark, so they won't hang around where there is artificial light. They also need pesticide-free gardens and some damper areas where there will be lots of small snails to feed on. Hedgerows and ponds seem to attract glow-worms, too. Look out for glow-worms on dark, moonless nights between late spring and early autumn. If you spot any in your garden, consider yourself very lucky, and try to keep conditions to their liking.

organising space

Left Cosy, enclosed areas help you feel secure in the garden at night, while also trapping and magnifying the scents of flowers.

Although there are different practicalities to put into place for different types of gardens, there are a few design constants that apply, particularly to a night garden.

Perhaps the most important is creating a sense of enclosure. Many people choose to leave their gardens open to their surroundings, making the most of borrowed views. An open, airy garden can be a lovely thing, but it doesn't make for the ideal night garden. If you want to make the most of night-scented plants, you have to close off the outside world and create a still pool of air where the fragrances will be trapped and will linger and mingle for as long as possible.

A sense of enclosure also helps to create a private, enveloping garden, somewhere you will feel safe and hidden away after dark. Tall, dense hedges such as yew (see p. 202) and box (see p. 183) should be your first line of defence. Grown along the boundaries of a garden, they provide a unity of background and create the feeling of a walled, secret garden, even if your garden doesn't have fabulous walls – or any walls at all. Hedges and taller trees planted around the boundaries will also filter much of the wind that attempts to blow away your night-time fragrances. Even in winter, bare tree branches will break the full force of any wind and will make your night-time winter garden a more inviting place to be, if only for ten or fifteen minutes at a time.

Dramatic silhouette plants such as cordyline (see pp. 186–187) and trachycarpus (see p. 203) also have their place in any night-time garden, whatever its purpose. Position some of these spiky, craggy plants on your garden's boundaries and enjoy the impressive shapes they make against the failing light of the evening sky.

what's your night-time garden style?

Before you start planning, look in detail at some of the different ways you might use your garden and therefore what features you might consider, or concentrate on, for each garden type. One of these night-time gardens is bound to be the garden of your dreams.

FRONT GARDENS

Imagine walking down the street of an evening, perhaps on your way out for a meal or on your way home from a late night at work. Suddenly you're enveloped in a cloud of intoxicating scent. You look around and spot one garden gleaming with pale flowers. That's where the scent is coming from. It is the sort of garden that you would make a small detour to walk past, one that would lift your spirits a little when you came across it.

The front garden is a hugely neglected space. All we do is walk through it when going from the house to the street and vice versa, and that's why people rarely expend any energy gardening in it. But it is also an area that sees a large amount of traffic and there may be many passers-by, particularly in the evenings as neighbours return from work and evening revellers head out. I always feel that a well-designed and cared-for front garden is a community-spirited thing. You may not be out there at night very often, but passers-by will appreciate any work you put in, particularly if you fill your front garden with night-scented plants that scent the street. And a beautiful front garden will help beautify the area, too, perhaps even inspiring neighbouring gardeners to create their own terrific gardens.

As I have said, the practicalities of a front garden are all about getting from the house to the street and vice versa as quickly as possible. To achieve this, you need a good, smooth path. You can make a pathway meander around pretty plantings, but chances are that the postman or newspaper delivery boy will find the shortest route to your front door, even if it means leapfrogging over a garden wall (especially the

Above Don't neglect front gardens. Scented plants such as Rosa 'Helenae' will be a treat to come home to.

newspaper delivery boy – the postman will want to, but will most probably stop himself). This means that a straight path from street to door is usually the best option.

You should also consider the lighting in your front garden. If you are near streetlights, you may get away without having any extra lighting, but if you're in a darker corner, you may want to consider installing a motion-sensitive light that switches on when you walk up the path. That way you can find the keyhole after an evening out. Alternatively, you could install some bollard lights along the pathway.

Making the most of your night-time front garden also means thinking about people you rarely consider – for example, the couple walking home after an evening out who sniff the air filled with the scent of night-scented stock, or the late-night dog-walkers who stop to admire your glowing lilies.

TINY BACK GARDENS AND BALCONIES

If you only have a tiny scrap of a back garden or a balcony – perhaps just space for a couple of chairs – you might think it's impossible to have an idyllic night-time garden. However, in some ways a balcony-sized patch makes the perfect night-time garden, particularly if you are short on time. For a start, it can be relatively easy to create privacy on a balcony. Pop up a garden parasol, place a couple of larger plants along the front, and you have your own leafy hideaway. Your options are limited to sitting, admiring and sniffing, with perhaps a little plant-tending, but that's not necessarily a bad thing.

In such a small space, detail is everything, so before you start on any plant- or furniture-buying, see if there is anything you can do to improve the look of the floor and walls. Sometimes just a lick of paint on the walls can make a huge difference. Paint them white or cream to reflect light, or terracotta if you prefer to create a cosier atmosphere.

In a small back yard, consider splashing out on some beautiful paving. You can afford the best as you won't need much of it. Because of the weight of paving, this won't be practical for a balcony, but if your balcony floor is made from ugly concrete, even painting it with a suitable outdoor paint will make it look better.

On a balcony and in a paved back yard, everything will have to be in pots. Choose a few really highly summer-scented plants, such as lilies (see pp. 98–99), zaluzianskya (see pp. 124–125), night-scented stock (see pp. 104–105), heliotrope (see p. 90) and mirabilis (see pp. 106–107), and plant each in its own pot. Then intersperse the pots with plenty of box-topiary shapes and big-boned plants such as trachycarpus (see p. 201) and cordyline (see pp. 186–187), again in individual pots.

So many plants in pots will mean lots of watering in summer, but this shouldn't be too hard to keep up with on such a small scale. However, you need to water daily at the height of summer and find someone to water for you if you go away on holiday or for a long weekend. You might want to think about installing a drip-irrigation system to make watering easier. This involves running a hosepipe fitted with drippers through your collection of potted plants, with one dripper per pot. You turn the tap on low and, 15 to 30 minutes later, everything has been watered. When you go away, you can put a timer between the tap and the hose so the water is turned on for a set amount of time each day.

Above Even a small balcony can offer you all the essential ingredients required for the perfect evening garden.

Make sure you leave space among the plants for a couple of chairs and a small table, even if it is only large enough to balance a couple of glasses and a lantern on.

Try to make use of any walls and ceiling, too – the roof of a pergola makes a good ceiling substitute. Attach hanging baskets full of flowing foliage to the ceiling and baskets full of petunias to walls. Look out, too, for wall-mounted candle holders and lantern-hangers.

You should also consider a water feature, even in the smallest area. Many, like wall fountains, are essentially just a small water tank and spout. Standing flush with a wall, they take up little space but look magnificent. Choose a classic design in which the water emerges from a lion's mouth into a small pool of water or the contemporary variation, with the water flowing over a sheet of stainless steel or glass, often into a completely invisible reservoir.

Overleaf Use large potted plants on a patio or balcony to create belts of shelter and privacy.

Plant lots of green, leafy plants around your wall fountain and, even when it is newly installed, it will look as if it has been there for decades. The gentle trickle of water can provide just the right level of comforting noise to distract you from the sounds of the street below or beyond, and can make your balcony or tiny back-yard patch a really special place to be in the evenings.

CONTEMPLATIVE GARDENS

Left A single chair will invite you to take a moment for yourself to stop and contemplate the beauty of the garden.

Perhaps you see your garden as a retreat from the world, from people and from noise and bustle; a place where, come evening, you can unwind, perhaps meditate or simply sit quietly in a comfortable chair with a drink by your side. If this vision of a quiet, contemplative twilight appeals to you, there are several things you can put in place to create it.

First, you will want to create a little privacy. This can be hard to come by in the back garden, particularly if you live in a built-up area. The windows of neighbouring houses will often directly overlook the patio or deck where you are sitting. Creating some kind of a canopy solves this problem instantly, particularly if it is mainly from above that you are overlooked.

You can put up a sail canopy simply and quickly, and it will instantly make your seating area feel as if it is nestling in its own little world. Bear in mind, though, that a sail canopy can also reduce light levels fairly severely in the house if it is placed too close.

Verandas are paved areas covered by a solid roof, which can be of glass. Verandas provide a good degree of privacy as well as great protection from the rain. Having a veranda means you can enjoy those warm but wet summer evenings as you sit in the dry, listening to the rain patter off the roof when everyone else in the neighbourhood has had to scuttle indoors. It makes the evening feel even more special when you know you're the only one who is out there enjoying it. The only drawback with verandas is that, in some areas, you will you have to seek planning permission to construct one. You will need to check with your local planning authority.

A pergola offers little protection from the rain and doesn't provide as solid a hideaway as a sail canopy, but it is relatively easy to erect, doesn't require planning permission, and lets through plenty of light. Plant yours up with climbing plants such as clematis (see pp. 134–135), honeysuckle (see pp. 102–103) and jasmine (see pp. 96–97), and it will quickly become more private. If the crossbeams of your pergola are placed far apart, string taut wires between them to give the climbing plants something to grow along. They will quickly provide a leafy roof for your seating area.

If privacy from upstairs onlookers isn't an issue, you may want to consider creating several areas for contemplation around the garden. Arbours and seats in the heart of the garden are far from the hustle and bustle of the household and can make perfect places to sit and

Right Plant arbours with night-scented plants such as *Lonicera periclymenum* 'Graham Thomas'.

think. Arbours are particularly good, as they provide some degree of privacy and you can make the most of their vertical surfaces by training night-scented climbers up them.

An area for quiet contemplation will be tricky to achieve if it is constantly assaulted by noise from outside the garden. The sound of vehicles and other comings and goings are difficult to avoid in built-up areas, so instead, concentrate on making your own relaxing noises within the garden to act as a distraction. This doesn't mean playing whale music at loud volume, though.

While you might not think that the gentle trickle of a waterfall could compete with the bleeping of the nearby pelican crossing, in fact this sort of constant, pleasant, low-level noise can be surprisingly effective. So consider installing a small, trickling water feature or, if you want something much easier to set up, you might think about hanging up wind chimes.

Personally, I can't abide tinkly wind chimes, but I'm quite fond of the wooden ones that clap and clank in a low-key, almost maritime fashion. Plants can join in, too. Bamboo (see p. 195) rustles beautifully in the slightest breeze, and will complement the clanking of wooden wind chimes perfectly. *Nandina domestica* (see p. 194) is known as 'heavenly bamboo', despite not actually being a bamboo at all. Its leaves make a particularly papery, rustling sound.

In a contemplative garden, you will want to keep the lighting low-key: lamps, lanterns and candles are particularly suitable if you are using the space for meditation. You will also want a comfortable set of chairs or even a wicker sofa to lie about on, and you might consider some big Middle Eastern-style cushions for really luxurious 'Arabian Nights' lounging. If you opt for these, though, you will also need a large, waterproof storage box or shed to throw them into at the end of the night or if rain threatens.

FAMILY GARDENS

A family garden has to be many things to many people, but if you have a young family and still want to be able to enjoy your garden in the evenings, storage should be high on your list of things to provide.

Large, sturdy storage chests with lids that double as seats are the perfect solution for families that want to be able to hurl all of the children's brightly coloured plastic toys out of sight come evening. You can buy these chests ready-made or have them custom-built in the form of long benches around the edges of a patio or deck. A sandpit with a good-looking wooden cover can also be perched on in the evening; they beat those sandpits with flimsy plastic covers hands down on looks, too.

If you use candles or lamps at night in your family garden, they need to be safely installed and out of reach of children, so consider hanging

Left Hammocks are the perfect family-garden feature, providing fun for children and relaxation for adults.

Right Eating out of doors can bring the family together, creating a fun and relaxed environment.

Overleaf Fill your garden with lanterns, tea lights and comfortable seats, mix some drinks and invite friends to enjoy the scene.

a few lamps from pergolas or buying wall-mounted candle holders. Older children often enjoy joining the adults in the garden in the evenings, and a barbecue or pizza oven is a great way to lure them out and get them interested in cooking outdoors. You can build either a barbecue or a pizza oven relatively cheaply and make it into a permanent feature of the garden, always ready for an evening of outdoor snacking.

Swing seats and hammocks are great choices for family gardens. They make for terrific fun in the daytime and convert to calm, restful and even romantic seats come evening. Large swing seats on frames aren't the most attractive thing, however; instead consider plain wooden swing seats that you could hang from a sturdy pergola or tree.

Lawns are a must in the family garden. Choose a hard-wearing seed mix (often labelled 'Family Lawn', or similar) that contains a high proportion of tough ryegrass. Keep the lawn well maintained to avoid it turning into a muddy mess.

entertaining

GARDENS FOR ENTERTAINING

Right For evenings
that will linger in the
memory, outdoor
events trump nights
indoors every time.

Maybe it's the fresh air; maybe it's the tension of wondering whether the whole shebang will have to be called off due to a freak rain shower, but an outdoor party is always more fun than an indoor one. If you regularly entertain in the house, consider creating a garden that will provide the perfect party or dinner-party venue.

There are obviously lots of practicalities to take into account. If you want to use your night-time garden mainly for entertaining, you will need to make sure you have a decent-sized patio or deck for your visitors to stand and sit on.

If you have the space, you might want a lawn, too, but holding even a dinner party on a lawn isn't a great idea. The table legs and stiletto heels of your fashionista friends will sink into a lawn, which is great for aerating it, but probably won't go down well when your girlfriends see the state of their Jimmy Choos afterwards.

Lawns also get damp and muddy, so they aren't great fun to hang about on. Plus, if you have lots of people standing on a damp lawn, it will become compacted and ruined. If you have space for both a lawn and a hard surface, then fine, but if it's a choice between the two and entertaining is your main aim, then go for the hard surface.

A patio or deck's the thing then. When you are planning one of these, allow as much space as possible; there is nothing worse than everyone squeezing around a table or teetering on the edge of a patio, fearing that you will topple into a flowerbed.

You will also need to invest in a good table and set of chairs. Hardwood is the best material for outdoor use, but make sure it is certified by the Forest Stewardship Council. This internationally recognised standard ensures that the wood used is sustainably harvested. If you are short on cash, you can make do with a salvaged household table and chairs, but do store them well over winter as they won't last as long. Covering the surface of the table in a patterned oilcloth or hammering on a sheet of zinc creates an unusual look and will make an indoor table last longer. If you throw large parties, you might consider putting in a number of small seating areas around the garden, where small groups of people can gather.

A permanent, brick-built barbecue or pizza oven makes a great focal point for a foodie party, while a fire pit with seating around will make it feel as if you're throwing a beach party. You can buy iron fire pits that can be stored away when not in use, or you could consider making a dedicated area for a fire pit. This should be a roughly

Above If you are interested in throwing dinner parties outdoors, invest in a beautiful, well-made dining table and chairs.

circular area on the ground, lined with stones, bricks or pebbles. The seating can be anything from a rough length of tree trunk to a smart bench; I would tend towards the rough tree trunk, as it suits the mood better. I would also site a permanent fire-pit area or brick-built barbecue away from the house, partly for safety reasons, but also so it is as far from the neighbours as possible. That way, you can sit up late and talk into the night without disturbing them.

You may also want to create some privacy; as much for your neighbours' benefit as for your own in the case of night-time garden entertaining. Consider canopy sails that shield late-night fun from upper windows, or surrounding seating areas with dense plants that will muffle sound if you are out late.

I always think that lighting for parties should be of the flame-and-fairy-lights variety. Fairy lights create just the right sort of atmosphere for entertaining and you can use them with abandon.

Flaming torches throw a very attractive light, but they need to be positioned with care so they don't catch on people's clothing. The perfect place for them is deep in borders, where they will look pretty but be well away from the revellers.

If your main interest in having a night-time garden is to use it as a party space, there is a good chance that you won't want to spend a great deal of time gardening. This doesn't mean that you shouldn't have decent-sized plant borders – most plants need very little attention once they are established – but to ensure a minimum of work, it is probably better to opt for more shrubs and fewer perennials. Choose strongly structural, low-maintenance plants such as cordyline (see pp. 186–187), choisya (see pp. 132–133) and trachycarpus (see p. 203), and intersperse them with a few pale, scented flowers. Trachelospermum (see pp. 120–121) needs a support to climb up, but once you provide that, it looks after itself pretty well. Night-scented hemerocallis (see p. 91) and evening primrose (see pp. 110–111) are good, low-maintenance perennial choices.

fireworks party

On a chilly Guy Fawkes Night, many of us wrap up warm and head off for a big local fireworks display. There will be masses of the noisiest, brightest and most beautiful fireworks, maybe even a musical accompaniment, some candy floss and a few fairground rides. But this isn't for everyone. Young children can find fireworks displays thrilling or they can be terrified, and when you are a child out in a big field far from your parents' car, there's nowhere to run if you start to get upset.

So what's the alternative? Bonfire night is a great excuse to have some fun in your garden at one of the darkest and bleakest times of year. Invite a few friends and their children round to enjoy an open fire and a small display of fireworks. Your visitors might even notice your winter-blooming plants in the flare of the Catherine Wheel.

A small fire is all you need to keep people cosy, and a fire pit is a great way to have a fire in the garden without scorching the grass (too badly). Get the fire going somewhere safe, with the children out of the way when you light it and where they can't get burned. Also make sure it is sited away from overhanging branches, the garden shed and the fence. Part-cook some baked potatoes, wrap them in foil and place

Above A small fireworks party gets you out into your garden at a time of the year when it is often ignored.

them around the edges of the fire in the embers. When you're ready to eat, fish them out carefully using barbecue tongs and eat them smothered with grated cheese. When it's time for dessert, furnish everyone with sticks and marshmallows to melt over the fire. Mulled cider will keep the adults warm; mulled or warmed apple juice will do the same for the children.

All fireworks shops sell selections that are suitable for small gardens, and you can even find boxes of quiet fireworks designed especially for people with pets or young children. They're still a bit noisy, obviously, but there won't be any big bangs or screeching.

Set up your fireworks area with a place for the audience that is well away from any danger. Make sure the children understand the importance of staying where they're told and appoint someone sensible and sober to put on the fireworks show. Children who find they don't like the fireworks can always sneak off and watch from the safety of an upstairs window. Oh, and don't forget to put the pets somewhere where they won't be frightened.

star or moon-gazing party

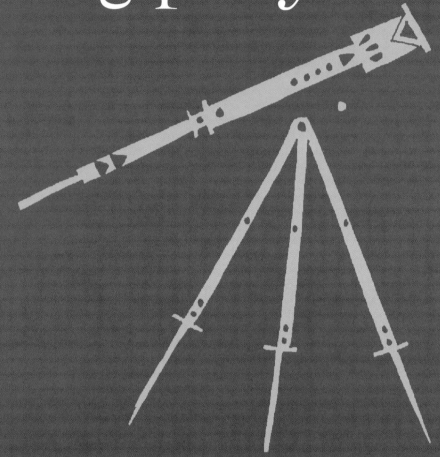

YOU WILL NEED

A telescope
Warm clothes
Hot-water bottles
Blankets
Hot chocolate
Rum
Soup
Chairs
A star map

If you have your own telescope, the night-time garden becomes a place you're drawn to again and again. Even a simple and fairly inexpensive bird-spotter's telescope turns your garden into an opportunity to make a connection with the heavens. A star-gazing or moon-gazing party can never be a guaranteed thing; you may have to cancel at the last minute as cloud decides to drift across your part of the planet, but that makes it all the more special and memorable for you and your guests when it does work.

To make a gazing gathering go with a swing, you need one of two things: a good moon or a celestial event. Of course, if you live in the countryside away from the light pollution that mars the sky at night, then it's worth simply setting up your telescope on a clear night, inviting your friends round and seeing what you can see. And don't forget your star map.

In the city, though, things are more limited. You can see the moon and you can spot shooting stars if you time your party to coincide with a meteor shower. Meteor showers occur all year round, but two of the most reliable are the Geminids in December, whose meteors produce flashes of yellow, blue, red and green among the white, and the Perseids in August, which shoot out up to 60 meteors per hour.

If you are moon-gazing, you really want the moon to be about half-full, or just over. When the moon is full, it's a bit glaring and hard to look at through a telescope, but when it's half-full, the shadows pick out all the craters. Even through a small telescope you get a wonderful sense of the heft and solidity of it. And keep your ear to the ground for news of lunar eclipses, too.

If you are star-gazing in the summer you won't have much trouble staying warm: you might need a jumper or two, and that's it. But in the winter, everyone needs to wrap up well. You don't want to light a fire to keep warm by and have its smoke cutting down on visibility. Instead, go for hot-water bottles, blankets, rum-spiked hot chocolate and soup. That should do the trick while your guests gaze at the stars in wonderment.

camping
in the garden

Your teenagers are at that awkward age: too young to go off camping on their own, but wanting to do something a little more exciting than just having friends round for the night in front of a DVD. On a warm summer evening, have them invite a few friends over and let them go camping in your garden. It will give them a taste of the freedom and fun of a real camping trip, but with mum and dad and the safety of the house just a few steps away should anyone get scared. They may think that camping in the garden sounds stupid, but if you can encourage them to give it a try, they are sure to have a truly memorable night.

Decide beforehand whether you're going to set up the tent yourself before anyone arrives, or if you are going to get the children to do it. Depending on who is involved, you will know what is likely to work best. The same applies to getting the campfire going. You should position this so there is no risk of setting fire to any vegetation or to your garden's shed or fences.

YOU WILL NEED

A tent
A fire pit
Torches
Camping mattresses
Rugs
Cushions
Sleeping bags
Sausages
Buns
Ketchup
Cans of drink
A midnight feast

Make the tent cosy with plenty of mattresses, rugs and cushions and use a few on the grass near the fire to keep everyone's bottoms dry. Have a few torches handy for when night falls.

The beauty of camping in the garden is that you don't actually have to cook out there if you don't fancy it. Your children will probably have more fun, though, and it's more in the spirit of camping if they cook over the campfire, so you will need to provide some food. Make it simple – food they can eat with their hands, like sausages or burgers in buns with ketchup, and some cans of drink.

Then you can let them settle down around the fire and chat, tell stories and play music until they're tired and crawl off to their sleeping bags. They may want to prolong the fun with a midnight feast, so remember to provide some food for that, too.

Don't get involved and keep well away – unless they come knocking in the middle of the night.

sundowner party

Epiphyllum oxypetalum is a plant with a fabulous capacity for bringing people together. Its secret lies in its fleetingness. It blossoms once a year and the blooms are incredible: huge, dinner-plate-sized and multi-petalled. It also has a rich, heady fragrance that is carried across the garden on the breeze. The flowers open from vast, pink buds, and they do it so quickly you can almost see the petals shuddering apart. A well-grown specimen can have many flowers all coming into bloom at once. It blooms only at night, with the flowers opening after dusk and fading before dawn. Then it's over, for another year.

The plant originates in the jungles of South America, but for some reason it is now widely grown in China and throughout the East. My own plant is a cutting from a huge plant that came from my stepfather's childhood home in Malaysia, and I have many memories of watching it open and sitting up as late as I was allowed to enjoy its seductive scent.

Wherever this plant is grown, it seems to be the cause of spontaneous sundowner parties. These spring up just as the *Epiphyllum oxypetalum* is about to launch into its one, passionate night of flowering. People sit and gaze and sniff the air in wonderment, then they gradually melt away into the night as the flowers start to fade. By morning, the flowers, which are considered a delicacy in China, where they are added to soups, hang limply from the plant.

Sundowner was also the name for a colonial tradition – a drink marking the passage from day into night. At the end of a long, hot day of ruling and pillaging, British colonialists in their various posts around the globe would gather with their neighbours to watch the sun go down and to relax with a long, cool drink. Gin and tonic was the ultimate sundowner, containing as it does malaria-beating quinine (in the tonic water), but other suitable sundowners are a Singapore Sling (gin, lime juice, cherry brandy and Benedictine) or a Cuba Libre (light rum, cola and a wedge of lime). Either of these would also make a suitably cooling, yet tropical, accompaniment to this sumptuous horticultural spectacle.

YOU WILL NEED

An *Epiphyllum oxypetalum* plant
A gin and tonic, Singapore Sling
or Cuba Libre

Above *Epiphyllum oxypetalum* has such impressive, highly scented and ephemeral flowers that its flowering is the subject of gatherings in Asia, where it is commonly grown.

summer barbecue

YOU WILL NEED

- A barbecue
- Barbecue tools
- Charcoal
- Matches
- Bunting
- Sausages
- Burgers
- Corn on the cob
- Salads
- Bread rolls
- Beer, chilled in a bucket of water
- Tables and chairs
- Napkins and paper plates
- Candles in jars

The ultimate occasion for enjoying and showing off your night garden is a summer barbecue. At this time of year, the weather is mild, the night-scented blooms are all doing their stuff, and you should have plenty of pale, summer flowers to impress your friends with as night falls. Good company, a few cold beers, and a beautiful setting make up for what is usually fairly mediocre food that is a bit burned around the edges and a bit raw in the middle. It's lucky that being outdoors makes you hungry.

Site your barbecue somewhere safe, where people can't knock it over, if it's the flimsy kind, and where you won't set fire to any overhanging vegetation or to a shed or the garden fencing.

The trick to a successful barbecue is to start it good and early. This gives enough time for the flames to lick away at the grill, then gradually subside, leaving just an ashy white covering to the coals. That's the time to start cooking. Put the grill in its highest position above the coals so the food cooks slowly through to the middle. Prepare for the chance of grilling disaster by having plenty of salads on hand and some tasty fresh rolls.

Above Throw a summer barbecue for a chance to show your evening garden off at its peak.

Bunting turns even the most average garden into an instant party location. You can buy bunting or you can make your own by cutting out triangles of fabric with pinking shears (which saves hemming) and sewing them to a length of ribbon. Then just string the bunting between fence tops and trees.

Most barbecues start in the afternoon and drift on into the evening, so lighting can be incidental. A few candles in jars here and there, scattered among your flowers, will provide enough of a glow to prevent people stumbling into your flowerbeds as the bucket of beer gets depleted.

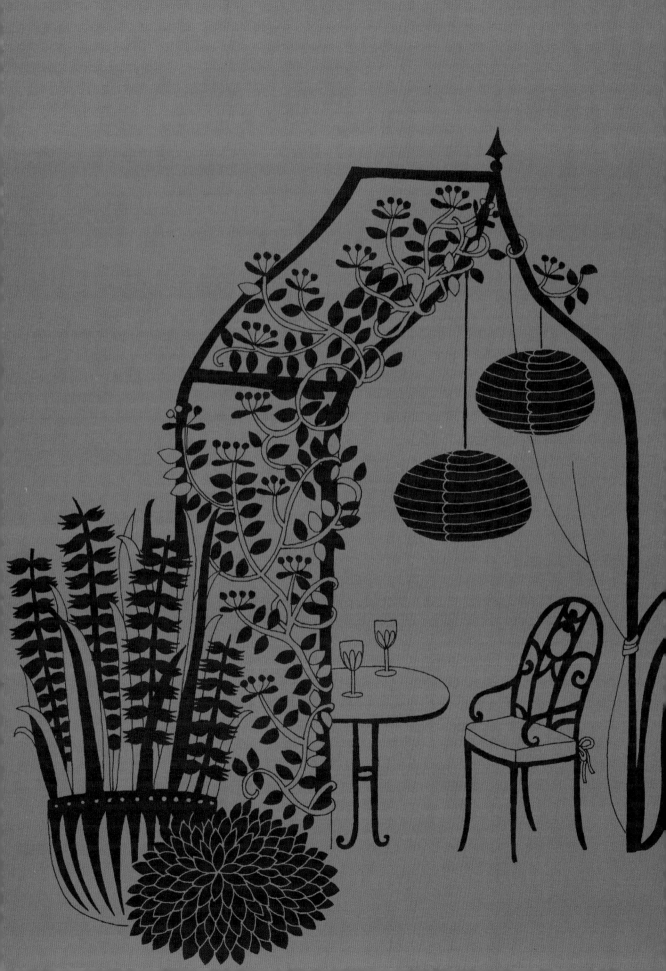

PART 2
PLANTS &
PLANTING

STAR PLANTS

The plants that will make your evening garden look special are those that are light-coloured or pure white. These will glow in the gloom of early evening or reflect back any glint of moonlight. The star plants in your evening garden should be these – lots of pale beauties to catch the eye after everything else has faded into the background.

But the evening garden is about all the senses; perhaps even more important than the sense of sight is the sense of smell. As darkness kicks in, all the plants in this section start to produce scent. A few are fresh with a citrus kick, but most are heavy and spicy, rich and intoxicating. These seem, appropriately enough, to be the scents of the night. Plant as many of these flowers as you can get your hands on. Each will add its own individual character to the evening breeze and will make your garden a place that you are constantly drawn to at night.

Brugmansia suaveolens
ANGEL'S TRUMPET

Situation	Full sun
Hardiness	Frost-tender (USDA zone 9)
Soil type	Any good potting compost
Height	3 m/9 ft 9 in
Spread	1.5 m/5 ft
Propagation	From cuttings in summer in a heated propagator, or sow seed in spring
Flowering period	Throughout summer and autumn

The scent of brugmansia (often commonly known as datura although not, strictly speaking, the same plant) is utterly intoxicating. It is said that if you fall asleep beneath one, you will have nightmares, and it's easy to understand why. The scent hangs in the air, heavy and penetrating. Brugmansia's common name is angel's trumpet, thanks to the huge, trumpet-shaped flowers that hang down dramatically from the stems. A well-grown plant covered in flowers is an extremely impressive sight. The flowers come in shades of red, orange, coral, pink, orange and white, with the white ones said to have the strongest scent.

However, all the flowers are so strongly scented that you needn't worry too much about the gradations between them. They are all completely over the top.

These vigorous plants will put on a good metre (3 ft) or even two (6 ft) of growth in a year in the right conditions, but they're not at all hardy so must be protected from frost. You will need a greenhouse that is kept at a minimum temperature of 7°C/44°F all winter. If you're not able to heat a greenhouse to this temperature, you could try bringing the plant indoors over winter. Ideally, you should place it in one of the cooler spots in the house, such as a minimally heated spare room. Only take it outdoors again once you are certain that all frosts have passed and the evening temperature is noticeably mild.

Plant brugmansia in a large pot in spring (remembering that you will need to be able to move the pot indoors again in the autumn) and use a good multi-purpose compost. Start watering and feeding as it comes into growth. To get the vigorous growth that will lead to the best flowering, give these plants huge amounts of water and feed them almost whenever you think of it; they will gobble it all up. As they grow, they send up forking stems. Don't prune these back as it is only after these stems are produced that the plants will flower.

Red spider mite can be a problem in dry weather. These tiny pests are barely visible so they are easy to miss. They suck sap from the leaves and slowly weaken the plant, discolouring the leaves and leaving a fine web across them. The mites thrive in dry conditions and hate humidity, so give the whole plant a regular watering (leaves and all) or mist with the fine nozzle on the hosepipe each evening to discourage them.

Be warned that all parts of the plant are poisonous.

Cestrum nocturnum
NIGHT-BLOOMING JESSAMINE

Situation	Full sun or partial shade
Hardiness	Tender; grow as a house plant (USDA zone 11)
Soil type	Moist but well-drained
Height	1 m/3 ft 3 in
Spread	1 m/3 ft 3 in
Propagation	From cuttings in autumn
Flowering period	Summer

This intensely, almost intoxicatingly, fragrant little plant needs to be grown as a house plant for most of the year, but it is worth the fuss. Commonly known as night-blooming jessamine, its unusual smell is quite unlike that of jasmine (the derivation of its common name) and more like a delicious spicy incense. It is widely planted in subtropical gardens, where it stays out all year long. Despite the plant's small stature, it has a very strong scent. It will waft across your garden, filling it with its tropical smell, while indoors it is so overwhelming that you will certainly want to move it outdoors for the summer.

Cestrum nocturnum is a small evergreen shrub with glossy, dark-green leaves. In summer it produces clusters of slender, tube-shaped whitish-green buds all along its stems, the ends of which open into little star-shaped, pure white flowers. Planted out in warmer climates, cestrum will grow to about 4 m/13 ft in height and spread. When you don't have the luxury of planting it in the soil, it is important to keep pruning it so that it's small enough to bring indoors as a house plant. The time to prune is just after the flowers have faded. Cut the stems back fairly hard, by about half, to stimulate new growth from lower down the plant and keep it bushy and compact.

Use a good peat-free multi-purpose compost and mix in plenty of grit to aid drainage. Water thoroughly throughout the summer and let the plant dry out almost completely before soaking it again. Feed once a week with a high-phosphate fertiliser such as tomato fertiliser or comfrey liquid. In winter keep the plant very dry and in a light, well-ventilated spot. You can keep it in a greenhouse or conservatory, but don't let the temperature drop below 5°C/41F°. If you can't manage this, keep it indoors in one of the cooler spots in the house.

Cestrums often drop their leaves in winter but, as long as you don't overwater them, they should leap back into life come spring.

Keep them out of reach of children or pets: all parts are toxic.

Citrus
CITRUS TREE

Situation	Full sun
Hardiness	Tender (USDA zone 11)
Soil type	Well-drained
Height	2 m/6 ft 6 in
Spread	1 m/3 ft 3 in
Propagation	From cuttings in summer
Flowering period	Mainly spring and summer, but can flower all year round
Fruiting period	Mainly in winter, but can fruit at other times

Citrus trees make beautiful, glossy little plants for a conservatory or patio. Their leaves are deep green and highly polished, and the white, waxy flowers, as well as the leaves, are sweetly citrus-scented. This is a plant that smells as strongly in the day as it does at night, but it adds a fresh, sharp note to other night-time scents.

Several of the citruses make particularly good pot plants. Lemons, limes and calamondins are the easiest to overwinter successfully, so these are the best choices for beginners. They're not hardy, though, so before any hint of a frost – ideally in about early autumn – you will need to put them in a frost-free greenhouse (heated to at least 4°C/40°F) and move them back outdoors for the summer. If you don't have a heated greenhouse, place your plant near a brightly lit window, ideally away from any radiators or direct source of heat.

It is a good idea to pot citrus trees on once a year into a slightly larger pot, top-dressing with fresh compost at the same time. One problem with this is that the plants get bigger and need larger and heavier pots, yet still need to be moved each year. A small trolley can be the solution: just make sure you place the tree onto the trolley while you can still lift it.

You can buy specialist citrus composts, but they are not really necessary. Instead, just add plenty of horticultural grit to the compost to keep it free-draining.

Citrus trees like a slightly acidic soil: if you want to avoid using a peat-based ericaceous compost, sprinkle sulphur chips on the surface of a normal compost. One of the problems that often besets citrus plants is yellowing of the leaves. This is caused either by the soil being too alkaline or by a lack of feed. Use a specialist citrus fertiliser every few weeks during the growing season. As well as keeping the plant well fed, it will help maintain the soil at the correct pH level.

Dianthus 'Mrs Sinkins'
PINK

Situation	Full sun
Hardiness	Hardy (USDA zone 8)
Soil type	Chalky/alkaline, well drained
Height	25 cm/10 in
Spread	30 cm/12 in
Propagation	From cuttings in summer
Flowering period	Early to midsummer

Pinks such as dianthus 'Mrs Sinkins' produce their delicious clove scent during the day, but the scent becomes even stronger at night. This isn't a plant that pumps scent out across the garden in the same way that, for instance, lilies do, but it will add a spicy layer to the scents of your night garden. Many of these dianthus are pale in colour, too, so they will stand out in the darkness.

Dianthus have been a favourite with gardeners from around the seventeenth century. They form neat mounds of grey-green foliage that make attractive ground cover and are a beautiful foil for other flowers even when they aren't in flower themselves. They come in colours ranging from white and pink through to crimson, maroon and blackcurrant, and many are patterned. 'Mrs Sinkins' is an old variety that has been in cultivation since 1868. In early and midsummer, it produces pure white double flowers that are prettily fringed at the edges and give out a particularly strong, rich scent.

Dianthus thrive in well-drained chalky soils and may struggle in a clay soil. Before planting in a heavier soil, mix lots of grit in and around the planting hole and add ground limestone. You may also need to put limestone around the roots regularly to keep the plant happy. These plants are drought-tolerant and will fare well in dryer areas, but they won't tolerate sitting in water and the stems will quickly rot. Plant them in a slight mound of soil so they are lifted above any standing water.

Consider using dianthus to edge your borders: they have a lovely low-growing habit and will spill out neatly over pathways. They can also be planted in gaps in paths or patios where, again, they will spill out over the paving. They look great in a Mediterranean border full of other silver-leaved plants, or in a gravel garden, but they're most at home in a cottage-garden border, planted towards the front. If you don't have the right type of soil, it is best to plant dianthus in containers rather than battle to make your soil suitable. You can then keep them near so you can enjoy the scent, or even put the pots on a table for your evening enjoyment. They do well in containers because they are drought-tolerant and can put up with a little neglect, but they will do best if you remember to water them frequently while they are in active growth. If you have them in pots, feed them regularly over summer with a balanced fertiliser. In the autumn, do a small tidy-up, cutting back long, straggling stems to make a neat mound that will look good all through winter.

Epiphyllum oxypetalum
QUEEN OF THE NIGHT

Situation	Dappled shade
Hardiness	Tender; grow as a house plant (USDA zone 11)
Soil type	Epiphytic cactus compost
Height	2 m/6 ft 6 in
Spread	1 m/3 ft 3 in
Propagation	From cuttings in spring
Flowering period	Late spring and summer

This magical plant often goes by the common name of queen of the night. It is the plant that has spawned a thousand sundowner parties (see pp. 72–73).

Epiphyllum oxypetalum is an epiphytic cactus, which means that, in the wild, it perches soil-less in the crooks of trees and similar spots. It has large, fleshy, rangy leaves and a quite crazy, untidy habit of growth, flinging stems and leaves out this way and that. You can try to contain it a little by wrapping a piece of garden twine around the stems to pull them together, but it really doesn't like to conform. It is also completely tender so can't be left outdoors all year round except in subtropical areas. This means you must grow it as a house plant in winter and can move it outside for summer. You can leave it indoors if you wish, but the scent can be quite overwhelming.

Epiphytic cacti have different needs from other cacti. Your average cactus wants a compost composed almost entirely of grit and to bake in full sun, whereas epiphytic cacti like a loose, low-nutrient compost with plenty of gaps in it – chunks of bark make a good addition. You can buy forest cactus compost or make your own from a mixture of sand, normal potting compost and part-composted bark chippings.

These cacti like dappled shade and will get burned in full sun. Once all chance of frost has passed, find them a spot outdoors, out of direct sun, for the summer. Water freely when in growth, particularly in hot weather. From early spring, apply a high-potash fertiliser such as tomato fertiliser or comfrey liquid to encourage flowering. Reduce the watering in winter, but don't let the plant dry out completely.

Cuttings take easily, particularly if struck in spring. Simply cut a leaf off and push it into a pot of compost mixed with sand or grit for drainage. Keep the pot somewhere warm and light but out of direct sunlight. A north- or east-facing windowsill is ideal. Keep the compost just moist. It has rooted when new shoots appear.

Heliotropium arborescens
HELIOTROPE, CHERRY-PIE

Situation	Full sun
Hardiness	Half-hardy; grow as an annual (USDA zone 10)
Soil type	Moist, well drained
Height	30 cm/12 in
Spread	20 cm/8 in
Propagation	Sow seed in early spring
Flowering period	Summer

Heliotrope is commonly known as cherry-pie because of its intense, sugary-sweet, vanilla-essence-like smell. The small purple flowers usually grow in a dome shape, but there are white-flowered forms, too, and these are even more strongly scented. The plant is strong-smelling both by daytime and at night.

Heliotropes are small, compact plants that look good in a summer bedding container or in a window box. They need a spot in full sun in order to flower at their best. They are actually short-lived, half-hardy shrubs, but it is tricky keeping them going from year to year, so they are most often grown as annuals. You may find them on sale as bedding plants in garden centres in spring. The purple-flowered, compact 'Marine' is the most commonly grown cultivar. 'White Lady' is one of the white-flowered cultivars.

Sow the seed thinly in early spring in a tray of levelled and firmed seed compost. Cover the seed with compost, then water in or sink the tray into a bath of water so it soaks water up. Let it drain, then place the tray in a heated propagator in good light. Prick the seedlings out into individual pots when they are large enough to handle. Plant them out only after you are fairly sure that the last frosts have finished. If you have a greenhouse, you can plant them into your outdoor mixed containers before the frosts are over and keep them there so they grow on and mingle with the other plants. If colder weather is forecast after you have put the containers outside, you can always swathe the entire pot in horticultural fleece to protect it. Water the plant freely when in growth and feed every couple of weeks with a general fertiliser.

A temperature lower than –2°C/28°F is likely to kill heliotropes, so if you want to overwinter them, you will have to keep them in a frost-free greenhouse. You can take cuttings in summer, but you'll have to overwinter these in a frost-free greenhouse. Keep any overwintering plants just moist: don't overwater.

Hemerocallis citrina

DAY LILY

Situation	Sun or partial shade
Hardiness	Hardy (USDA zones 3–9)
Soil type	Moist, humus-rich
Height	1 m/3 ft 3 in
Spread	75 cm/30 in
Propagation	From divisions in spring or autumn
Flowering period	Early to midsummer

A plant with the common name of day lily might not seem an obvious choice for an evening garden, but the name refers to the fact that each of the day lily's flowers opens for just 24 hours or less. Most open in the day and fade towards night, but the flowers of *Hemerocallis citrina* open in mid-afternoon, are in full bloom by evening and continue through the night. It produces a mainly lemony scent, with hints of honeysuckle. The flowers fade early the next day, but throughout midsummer there is always a succession of buds waiting on the prolific flower stalks.

The flowers are fine and delicate, with thin, pale yellow petals. They are arranged in a star-like fashion, slightly recurved at the tips. The pale yellow shows up well in low light.

Day lilies form generous clumps of long, thin, shiny, strap-like leaves. They are herbaceous perennials, so they die down over the winter. Spring and autumn are when you should lift and propagate them. Use your garden fork to loosen the soil around the plant, then lift the whole clump. Plunge two forks back to back into the centre of the clump to prise it into two pieces. You can either replant the pieces immediately or pot the divisions in containers of fresh compost. Do this every few years whether you want to propagate or not, as clumps will flower less as they get larger and more congested.

Day lilies like a rich, fairly moist soil. They grow well in partial shade, but produce more flowers in full sun. Remove the individual spent flowers to encourage more flowers to form as well as to keep the plant looking tidy. When all the buds on a flower stalk have opened and faded, cut the stalk right back to its base. When the leaves have died back you can pull them off. Mulch all around the plant with a thick layer of compost or well-rotted farmyard manure in spring. If it is to form the maximum number of flower buds, the day lily's roots need to be moist throughout spring, so start watering when growth first starts and continue throughout spring if the weather is dry.

Hesperis matrionalis
SWEET ROCKET

Situation	Sun or partial shade
Hardiness	Hardy (USDA zones 3–9)
Soil type	Humus-rich but well drained
Height	90 cm/36 in
Spread	45 cm/18 in
Propagation	Sow seeds in spring
Flowering period	Late spring to late summer

Sweet rocket lives a double life. During the day, it is the perfect, sweet, pretty cottage-garden plant. It rubs along beautifully with other cottage-garden perennials and attracts bees and insects – especially butterflies – from all around. Come evening, its strong, spicy scent kicks in and spreads throughout the garden. You will quickly find that moths love it just as much as butterflies do. As well as the name sweet rocket, it has a number of other common names, many of which allude to its smell or its place in the evening garden. These names include dame's violet, damask violet, eveweed and mother-of-the-evening.

Sweet rocket was first grown in England in the sixteenth century, which is perhaps why it looks so completely at home in a cottage-garden setting. Plant it with alliums, hardy geraniums and roses to pull off the complete cottage-garden look with ease.

The species *Hesperis matronalis* is a pretty biennial or short-lived perennial that bears loose panicles of pale pink or purple flowers on tall stems throughout summer, from late spring well into late summer. *H. m.* var. albiflora is the white-flowered version and smells just as good, with the added bonus that the flowers show up better at night. Both last well as cut flowers, so if the summer weather isn't good and you are not managing to sit out and enjoy the evening scents, you can at least cut yourself a few sprigs to enjoy indoors.

Being a short-lived perennial, your plants will start to fade away after a few years and the flowers will gradually become fewer and fewer. Luckily, this plant self-seeds with abandon. All you need to do is thin out the seedlings to allow a few plants to grow full-size each year, and you will have them in perpetuity. If you want to move self-sown seedlings to a new part of the garden, do so whenever they are large enough to handle easily. If you find they're becoming a pest and you want to stop them self-seeding, try to remember to cut off the spent flower spikes before they go to seed.

Should you want to start new plants from seed, you should sow a thin row in spring on a spare patch of soil or in a nursery bed that has been well worked and raked to form a fine tilth. When the seeds germinate, thin them out to around 30 cm/12 in apart. Transplant them to their final planting places in autumn and the plants will start flowering in the summer of the following year. New plants will need watering in dry weather while they are getting established.

In their native habitat, these plants are woodland dwellers and can tolerate partial shade or full sun. The soil should be moist but well drained and should echo the soil found in a woodland setting, which means that it should contain plenty of organic matter. Leaf mould makes the perfect addition to the soil and will help keep the plants happy and their roots moist.

Ipomoea alba
MOONFLOWER

Situation	Full sun or partial shade
Hardiness	Tender; grow as an annual (USDA zone 10)
Soil type	Fertile, well drained
Height	4 m/13 ft
Spread	2 m/6 ft 6 in
Propagation	Sow seed in spring
Flowering period	Summer to autumn

The moonflower, *Ipomoea alba*, is a vigorous twining climber that clambers up supports. It has large, dark green leaves and produces huge, white, trumpet-shaped blooms. The flowers stay tight shut against the sunshine during the day, then open at night in a swift movement, taking only about a minute to unfurl. Once open, they emit a strong, sweet, moth-attracting fragrance.

Moonflower grows quickly to cover a support, but it isn't hardy so will only last one season. Despite growing as a perennial in warmer countries, in colder climates it is most often grown from seed each spring as an annual. The seed coat is hard, so the seed can be slow to germinate. To soften the coat, soak it in tepid water for a few hours before sowing. If the seed is particularly large and tough, nick it with a knife or rub it onto sandpaper to break through the seed coat before soaking it. Sow several seeds to a pot or scatter them across a seed tray filled with seed compost. Cover with compost and water in.

When the seeds have germinated, transplant them into individual pots of fresh compost. Keep them well watered in a warm, light spot. You can plant them out once all danger of frosts has passed, either direct into the soil or in a large container filled with peat-free multi-purpose compost. Wherever you put them – but especially if they are in the ground – you will need to take care to protect them from slugs. Keep the plant well watered throughout summer and feed every couple of weeks with a high-potash fertiliser such as tomato fertiliser or comfrey liquid. At the end of the season, the plant will be killed off by the cold weather.

Although this plant is an annual, it's a big one (you could use it to hide an ugly wall) and needs a strong support, such as a wooden trellis or system of wires, to clamber up. To begin with, you will have to tie the first growths loosely to the support to help the tendrils attach to it. They are unlikely to need any more help than that, but check from time to time and tie in more growths if necessary.

Jasminum officinale

JASMINE

Situation	Full sun or partial shade
Hardiness	Frost-hardy to –5°C/23°F in a sheltered spot (USDA zone 7)
Soil type	Humus-rich, slightly moist
Height	12 m/ 39 ft 4in
Spread	10 m/32 ft 9 in
Propagation	From cuttings in summer
Flowering period	Summer

Jasmine's long, fine, deep green stems twine up a support. In summer it is smothered in small, pure white, star-shaped flowers, which show up well against the dark background created by the fine leaves. You might even call the plant delicate if it weren't quite such a romper. Jasmine is a truly vigorous plant once it gets going. It will cover a pergola in no time and can even be used to clothe a small garden building or to help you disguise an ugly fence or wall.

The flowers emit a strong, sweet fragrance that is particularly strong in warm, sheltered spots. In fact, you will have to choose the sunniest and most sheltered spot in your garden for this plant, as jasmine is only hardy to around –5°C/23°F, so it will struggle in harsher winters. Tucked away in a warm, sunny corner, the plant will fare better.

The plant is semi-evergreen or deciduous, so it will keep some of its leaves during milder winters. Don't expect it to provide a great deal in the way of evergreen winter structure, however; jasmine has a tendency to look pretty ropey in winter, although it quickly leaps back to life come spring.

Jasmine needs a sturdy support to climb up. A set of parallel wires fixed to a wall or a chunky trellis will be perfect. You may need to help it start climbing up a pergola, so tie the shoots in loosely to begin with. Then, once the plant has wrapped itself around the pergola supports sufficiently, you can remove the ties.

The main problem with jasmine is keeping it under control. It grows extremely quickly and will outgrow all but the very largest of supports if not pruned occasionally. The best time to prune is just after flowering. Bear in mind that flowers are borne on stems that are at least a year old. In other words, if you cut the plant back completely, you will have a whole year to wait until the stems are mature enough to bear flowers.

When pruning, aim to remove up to one-third of the oldest flowered stems each year. If the plant has become completely overgrown and this seems too fiddly, you can chop it back hard. If you do this, do it in spring and give it plenty of mulch, feed, water and care afterwards.

Jasmine likes a soil that contains plenty of moisture, but doesn't like to sit in water over winter. Before planting, improve the soil with plenty of organic matter such as leaf mould to keep the soil moist but free-draining. Mulch with leaf mould or garden compost once a year.

Lilium regale 'Album'

LILY

Situation	Full sun
Hardiness	Hardy (USDA zone 8)
Soil type	Rich and fertile but well drained
Height	1.5 m/5 ft
Spread	30 cm/12 in
Propagation	Lift bulbs in autumn and separate offsets to grow on
Flowering period	Midsummer

Lilies provide one of the must-have scents of the summer – rich and sweet and at its strongest and most delicious on a warm evening. Their tall stems reach up above other perennials and the large, trumpet-shaped flowers gaze down elegantly over the garden. A good-sized clump of these pure white lilies is a majestic sight and will fill the evening garden with scent.

Lilium regale has white flowers, but the backs of the petals are pink. *L. r.* 'Album' is exactly the same shape, but with petals that are entirely white and with a particularly strong fragrance. Asiatic and Oriental lilies really need to be planted into containers, but *L. regale* and its cultivars are surprisingly tough and can be planted out in the garden where they'll slowly clump up. Plant them among clumps of perennials.

Buy the lilies as bulbs in spring or autumn. It can be hard to get hold of lilies in autumn, but if you can find them and get them planted at that time of year, the roots get a chance to develop during the winter and you will get a better display in the first year. On the other hand, there is generally a better choice of bulbs in spring.

Choose a planting spot where the bulbs and roots will get some shade but where the growth and flowers will be in full sun. A spot among ground-cover perennials such as hardy geraniums is perfect. The soil needs to be rich and moist, but water must drain away easily as the bulbs won't put up with sitting in water over the winter. Adding a mix of compost, leaf mould and grit to the planting hole will ensure you get the balance right. If you are planting in a container, put plenty of crocks in the base to ensure the drainage hole doesn't get blocked with compost, then use a mixture of good, peat-free multi-purpose compost and grit.

Whether in pots or in the soil, you should plant the bulbs as early in the year as you can manage and you should plant them deeply, with about 12 cm/5 in of soil above them. After flowering, feed with a high-potash fertiliser such as tomato fertiliser or comfrey liquid. This will help build them up for the following year. If you are growing your lilies in pots, it is important to keep them evenly watered while they are in leaf, as drought can affect flowering.

The main problem that afflicts lilies is the red lily beetle. This beautiful scarlet fiend lays its eggs on the undersides of the foliage. As the grubs hatch and grow, they cover themselves in a brown sticky substance and start eating away at the leaves. An unnoticed infestation can strip the foliage in a few days. Inspect the undersides of leaves regularly for rows of red eggs and for the grubs, and squash them on sight. Kill the adults, too, when you spot them.

Lonicera japonica 'Halliana'

HONEYSUCKLE

Situation	Partial shade
Hardiness	Hardy (USDA zones 4–9)
Soil type	Moist, humus-rich
Height	10 m/32ft 9 in
Spread	3 m/9 ft 9 in
Propagation	From cuttings in summer
Flowering period	Summer

If you're the generous sort and want to give your neighbours as magical an experience of night-time gardening as you are planning for yourself, trying planting honeysuckle. It is the ultimate evening garden plant, producing great wafts of honey-like scent that permeate the summer evening air. If it is allowed to really romp away and clamber up a large tree or over a sturdy pergola, honeysuckle will perfume the air of the entire neighbourhood. Planting one is a truly benevolent act.

The flowers are made up of clusters of long, tubular flowers that bear the scent. As a rough rule of thumb, the less showy the flowers, the greater the scent. This means that the pale yellow flowers of *Lonicera japonica* 'Halliana' release one of the strongest scents, yet the vivid orange and red *L. j.* 'Dropmore Scarlet' is almost entirely unscented. Unfortunately, you have to choose between looks and smell. That's not to say that the scented honeysuckles are ugly, but they are not fine and delicate, so they look their best in a woodland or cottage-garden situation.

Honeysuckles are, in fact, originally woodland plants. This makes them quite handy in the garden since they can tolerate a fair bit of shade. If you want something that will cover a north- or east-facing wall and still produce flowers, honeysuckle is a good bet.

Honeysuckle climbs by means of lax, twining stems rather than with suckers, so it needs quite a bit of help to get it moving skywards. This means you will need to provide a support system. A trellis (but not one with small squares, as the honeysuckle's long stems can't weave their way through) offers reasonable support, but not once the honeysuckle really gets going. Parallel wires stretched across a wall approximately 30 cm/12 in apart work much better. Choose good, thick wire for the job: once the honeysuckle gets big and heavy, it will quickly pull thinner-gauge wire out of place. During the growing season, you should regularly tie the stems to the support, or at least twine them around it if they are not doing so themselves. Since honeysuckle is a woodland plant, it will appreciate a moist, humus-rich root run. Use plenty of leaf mould or compost in the planting hole and mulch with more of the same once a year.

Honeysuckle often suffers from powdery mildew – a fungus that manifests as a white powdery coating on the leaves. It occurs when the roots become dry. Unfortunately this happens fairly often with climbers that are planted near walls and fences, as these cast a 'rain shadow' that prevents rain from reaching the soil. So plant your honeysuckle as far away from the wall as possible and lean the plant into it. Remember to water it in dry weather.

Matthiola bicornis
NIGHT-SCENTED STOCK

Matthiola incana
BROMPTON STOCK

Situation	Full sun
Hardiness	Hardy annual (USDA all zones)
Soil type	Fertile, slightly moist
Height	35 cm/14 in
Spread	25 cm/10 in
Propagation	Sow seeds in spring
Flowering period	Summer

The annual night-scented stock, *Matthiola bicornis*, isn't much to look at in the daytime. The pale greenish-grey stalks and leaves are fairly sparse and the plant can look a bit rangy. The flowers are even slightly shrivelled. But as night falls, the petals unfurl and you get small, pink or pale purple star-shaped flowers that pump out a spicy clove-and-vanilla scent that fills the garden. Because of their slightly wild appearance, these stocks look best combined with other plants in a cottage-garden border, rather than in a container where they would look a little sparse, particularly during the day.

As an annual, this stock should be sown in spring. You can sow it direct where it is to flower and thin it out later, but you will achieve better results if you sow into a seed tray or small pot and pot it on or thin it out later. The seedlings are very small and you may need to pot them on in small clumps, rather than trying to pot them on individually. Plant out as soon as the plants are large enough.

M. bicornis will self-seed fairly readily if it finds a spot to its liking, so if you want it to return, make a point of learning what the seedlings look like so you can avoid them when you're doing the weeding.

M. incana is a short-lived perennial that is also sweetly scented. It produces short, stout flower spikes smothered in four-petalled flowers. There are many pretty cultivars that are useful as bedding plants for the evening garden. Some of these are double and so create a fuller, more voluptuous effect than the annual stock, although the scent isn't as impressive. They are available in a range of strong pinks and purples through to paler colours. Their stature and colour make them a great choice for a summer container in a twilight garden.

If you're lucky, you might find the perennial stock in the bedding section of your garden centre, among the bedding geraniums and lobelias. But you can't always rely on this, so if you are keen to feature this plant in your twilight garden, you would do best to grow it from seed, just as you would night-scented stock (see above). Make sure you grow the perennial stock in plenty of light so that the plants don't become leggy.

Both plants require a warm, sunny position to grow at their best, and they prefer to be sheltered from the wind, too.

Mirabilis jalapa

MARVEL OF PERU, FOUR O'CLOCK PLANT

Situation	Full sun
Hardiness	Frost-hardy (USDA zone 9)
Soil type	Well drained
Height	60 cm/24 in
Spread	60 cm/24 in
Propagation	Sow seed in spring or from divisions in spring
Flowering period	Throughout summer

Mirabilis jalapa, which goes by the impressive common name of marvel of Peru, is one of the few night-scented plants with colourful flowers. But if you think this would make it good for bringing a splash of daytime colour to a garden designed for evening, you'd be wrong. Its other common name is four o'clock plant: the flowers stay tightly closed until late afternoon, then the cool of the evening triggers them to open. The flowers are vibrant deep pink, paler pink, yellow and white, all on the same plant, and they can change colour as they age – yellow to pink, white to purple. They're also strongly fragrant, with a sweet, orange-blossom-like scent. Come morning, the individual flowers wither and die, but throughout summer there is always a succession of flowers waiting to bloom the following evening.

These are perennial plants that are just about frost-hardy, meaning that they will survive a fall in temperature to –5°C/23°F. The first light frost cuts the top growth down. The tuber that is left in the ground may survive the winter, particularly in mild areas and if the ground has been covered in a thick, dry mulch, such as bark chippings, after the plant has died back. Alternatively, you can lift the tuber after the first frosts and overwinter it as you might a dahlia tuber. Brush off the dirt, nestle it in some sawdust or vermiculite and store it in a dark, frost-free place until early spring. Then bring it out, plant it up and water it, keeping it in a frost-free place until all danger of frost has passed.

But mirabilis will grow quickly and flower freely in its first year when grown from seed, and that is how it is usually treated. The seeds are large and germinate easily. Sow them in early spring in a frost-free place, pricking them out into individual pots when they are large enough to handle and planting them out after the last frosts. Choose a spot that receives full sun, is sheltered and has a reasonably well-drained soil. Alternatively, you can plant them into containers, which will allow you to bring them up close to seating areas where the scent can be appreciated. In autumn it is easy to save the big, black seeds for growing the following year. Store these in a cool, dry place.

When the plants are young, the new growth is particularly susceptible to aphids. Check young plants frequently and squash any aphids you see. If you get a bad infestation, it can really slow growth, particularly when the plant is young and just getting going. Frequent misting of the plant with a very mild detergent solution (a small drop of washing-up liquid to a mister of water) can help keep aphids under control.

Nicotiana sylvestris

FLOWERING TOBACCO

Situation	Full sun or partial shade
Hardiness	Half-hardy annual (USDA zone 8; annual elsewhere)
Soil type	Moist, woodland-type soil
Height	1.5 m/5 ft
Spread	50 cm/20 in
Propagation	Sow seeds in early spring
Flowering period	Throughout summer

Nicotiana is possibly the most famous night-scented plant. With its huge, 1.5 m/5 ft spires of dangling white flowers, it makes a massive impact in the night garden and would be an impressive plant even without its scent.

One of the most remarkable things about *Nicotiana sylvestris* is that it's an annual. This means that it has to put on massive amounts of growth, produce bucketfuls of flowers and, if you let it, seed – and all in a few short months.

To give it the best chance, you need to start the small seeds off good and early in the spring. Sow them on the surface of a fine, well-sieved seed compost and water in. Ideally, place the seed trays or pots in a heated propagator to ensure good germination. Grow on in a greenhouse and, when the weather gets warmer, slowly harden the plants off by putting them outdoors during the day and bringing them back indoors at night. You should eventually plant them out in the garden around late spring.

At first, the plants will form a rosette of paddle-like leaves, then the huge flower spikes will start to emerge. These will be topped with green buds that open to reveal pure white, star-shaped, drooping flowers with improbably long, thin necks. These prove much too delicate for the job, so the flowers dangle gracefully, unable to hold their heads up. The effect is like a particularly classy, pure white firework.

Children love this plant: it towers over them, jungle-like, with its huge leaves and explosions of flowers. Thanks to its sticky, hairy leaves, it also gets plastered in tiny,

dead flies. This goes down well with kids who are attracted to all things gruesome; less well with children of a more sensitive disposition. During the day, it smells of nothing, so children usually miss out on the big show. By dusk, the scent starts to kick in, sweet and strong and, as night deepens, it only gets stronger. Moths love these flowers, using their long proboscises to probe deep down the dangling throats and access the nectar held at the base of the flowers.

Plant nicotiana in full sun in soil that has been well prepared with lots of garden compost or well-rotted farmyard manure. Choose a fairly sheltered spot, out of strong winds, for the tall stems can be blown over or end up leaning if the wind is strong. You can stake any plants that are having trouble staying upright by pushing a bamboo cane firmly into the soil and then tying the flower stalk loosely onto it with twine. Cut off faded flower heads to encourage new flushes of flowers, but leave some flowers on if you want them to self-seed.

Oenothera biennis

EVENING PRIMROSE

Situation	Sun
Hardiness	Hardy (USDA zone 4)
Soil type	Well drained
Height	1 m/3 ft 3 in
Spread	60 cm/24 in
Propagation	Sow seeds direct or in pots in early summer
Flowering period	Early summer to early autumn

The yellow flowers of the evening primrose open late in the day, as evening falls, and they do so surprisingly swiftly. They're loved by both day-flying insects, such as bees and butterflies, and by night-flyers such as moths. In the evening it's their sweet perfume that mainly attracts pollinators, and it is this that makes it worth growing in the twilight garden. The evening primrose produces tall flower spikes, each bearing many cup-shaped flowers along its length. The flowers open pale yellow and age to a darker yellow with a hint of green. This colour combination makes them really luminous in low evening light, although the younger flowers glow the most brightly.

Evening primroses are at their best when planted in well-drained sandy soil, since heavy clay soils can lead to rotting during the winter. If you have to plant them in heavy soil, mix plenty of grit into the planting hole as well as into the area around it, to allow water to drain away. They like plenty of nourishment, too, so dig lots of compost or well-rotted manure into the soil.

Being a biennial – which means it will grow leaves in its first year, flower in its second year, then die – evening primroses should be propagated from seed in early summer. Sow them any earlier than this, and the plant may get large enough to attempt to flower, but it will be a weak and puny attempt and will stop the plant from growing big and beefy for a great show the following year. Sowing in early or midsummer should be perfect.

The seed is very fine indeed. It can be sown direct where it is to grow, then thinned out later, or sown thinly onto the surface of soil in pots, then thinned out. In autumn, the young plants should be put in their final planting positions and kept well-watered while they get established. They will flower from midsummer the following year.

Cut back the flower spikes as they go over. Once the final flower has finished, you can either leave it in place and allow seeds to form, in which case it is very likely to self-seed, or you can pull the whole plant out and compost it.

Despite being short-lived, since evening primrose self-seeds so readily, you should always have a succession of younger plants coming along. Once it has decided it likes your garden, you are unlikely to need to do much to encourage it. In fact, it can become a bit of a weed, albeit a very lovely one. The best way to prevent it becoming too much of a problem is to snip off the flower spikes before they have a chance to go to seed.

Petunia Tumbelina series
PETUNIA

Situation	Full sun
Hardiness	Half-hardy (USDA zone 10; annual elsewhere)
Soil type	Moist, well drained
Height	40 cm/15 in
Spread	30 cm/12 in
Propagation	Sow seed in spring
Flowering period	Summer

Petunias aren't the most highly esteemed plants. Classier gardeners regard them as a bit common and brash – not quite the thing. That may be because they are so popular and are often used in bright, clashing colour mixtures. Come spring, they are on sale in every garden centre and in summer they seem to be in every hanging basket and bedding scheme.

In fact, petunias are extremely floriferous, hard-working plants. They're also night-scented (some smell in the daytime, too, but you have to get really close and have a good sniff). In the evening they emit a faint scent, but they really come into their own in the dead of night, when they produce wafts of sweet vanilla-like scent. They might be most appreciated by late-night revellers returning home in the small hours.

Petunias are the mainstay of any summer bedding display. They have a very attractive habit, with trailing stems that are absolutely smothered in trumpet-shaped or frilly double flowers all summer long. You can completely plant a hanging basket or container with petunias or you can make the most of their trailing habit by using them to soften or even hide the edges and sides of a mixed container.

Avoid the clashing-colour problem by choosing your petunias carefully. A container of pale petunias combined with the silvery foliage of the bedding plant *Senecio cineraria* 'Silver Dust', for instance, is perfect for a twilight garden.

The Tumbelina and Wave series are among the more highly scented petunias. You may struggle to track these down at planting-out time, so you may prefer to grow them from seed. Sow in early to mid-spring. The seed is really tiny and hard to handle, so mix a small amount with a teaspoonful of silver sand, then sprinkle the mixture onto the surface of a seed tray filled with firmed, levelled and wetted compost. Don't cover with compost. Place in a heated propagator in a well-lit place. When the seeds have germinated, pot them on in small clumps then, when these are large enough to handle, pot them on into separate modules.

When all danger of frost has passed, you can plant the modules – as well as any garden-centre plants – in your outdoor containers, but be ready to protect them with fleece if there are warnings of late frosts.

If you have a greenhouse, you can pot up your outdoor containers fairly early in the spring and grow them on in the greenhouse so they look full when you put them outside.

Polianthes tuberosa

TUBEROSE

Situation	Full sun
Hardiness	Frost-tender (USDA zone 9)
Soil type	Well drained but moist
Height	90 cm/36 in
Spread	15 cm/6 in
Propagation	From offsets in autumn
Flowering period	Summer

The tuberose is possibly the most strongly scented of all the night plants. It has an intense, heavy, decadent fragrance that is produced by tall spikes of thick, waxy, star-shaped, double, pure-white flowers. The plant would be worth growing for its exotic beauty alone, even if it didn't smell delicious. The cultivar 'The Pearl' has an even stronger fragrance than the species; in fact, it's almost a bit much.

One of the tuberose's common names is mistress of the night. It will make you work hard for its scent, though: it's a bit of a diva and certainly isn't a plant you can throw in the ground and forget about.

Hailing as it does from Mexico, it's not surprising that the tuberose likes a bit of heat. It can be left to grow in a pot all summer if you like, then it can easily be moved indoors when the weather turns colder. Either way, to get the best out of it, it needs to be in your warmest, sunniest spot all summer long.

When you first plant the tubers out and they're just starting into growth, they need a lot of moisture, so water frequently and deeply. This will encourage the flowers to form. When the plant is in growth, water in some liquid fertiliser every two weeks. Once the main plant has flowered it won't flower again, so you'll need to remove the small offsets that appear on the main plant and grow them on. Plant each offset on into a small pot of fresh compost and keep well watered until growth starts to slow in autumn. If they're going to flower the following year, they need as long a period of growth as possible – ideally at least four weeks – before they start to go into dormancy in autumn. When this happens, the leaves will shrivel and yellow. At this point, slowly reduce watering until the soil is completely dry. Keep it dry throughout winter.

Tuberoses needs warmth – at least 15°C/59°F throughout winter – so a greenhouse that is just frost-free isn't likely to be sufficient. You may be better off overwintering them in the house.

Saponaria officinalis
SOAPWORT

Situation	Full sun or partial shade
Hardiness	Hardy (USDA zone 4)
Soil type	Well drained; tolerates poor soils
Height	30 cm/12 in
Spread	20 cm/8 in
Propagation	From divisions in autumn
Flowering period	Summer into autumn

Common soapwort, sometimes also known as bouncing bett, is an easy-to-grow hardy perennial with pale pink flowers that release a sweet scent at night. Hailing as it does from meadows and rocky, mountainous areas, this is a useful plant that grows well in poor, gravelly soils. In fact, soapwort is best confined to such soils as there is a risk of it becoming invasive in gardens where the soil is too rich.

There are some more compact, less invasive cultivars, but soapwort is generally a big grower so is best planted where it can spread to its heart's content and alongside strong, vigorous neighbours, such as Japanese anemones. They are definitely worth growing, though. They look good in borders with other cottage-garden perennials, are hugely floriferous, and will create an incredible bank of night fragrance with no trouble at all.

Plant soapwort in spring or autumn in well-drained soil in full sun or partial shade. If you are planting in the spring, keep well watered, particularly during dry spells, until the plants are established. If you are planting in autumn, you may need to water a little until the plants die down for winter, but after that they will probably take care of themselves.

Soapwort has a fairly floppy growth habit, so it is a good idea to have some support in place around the plants before the new shoots emerge in spring. This is better than supporting them once they have grown large: perennials supported later on always look rather trussed-up and awkward. You can use plant-support rings or bamboo canes or simply use any shrubby prunings that are left over from your winter pruning.

After flowering, deadhead the plants, cutting back into the stems a little. This encourages growth from the base, keeps the plant from flopping too much, and sometimes leads to a second flush of blooms.

Perennials like this one die down in winter, leaving dead stems behind. You can leave these on the plant or cut them back to tidy the plant up for winter, but it is now generally regarded as good practice to leave the dead stems on so insects can overwinter on them. You can, however, have a little snip every now and then if they get too messy. Cut all stems down to the ground in spring.

It is simple to propagate soapwort from divisions in autumn.

Trachelospermum jasminoides
STAR JASMINE

Situation	Full sun or partial shade
Hardiness	Frost-hardy to –5°C/23°F in a sheltered spot (USDA zone 7)
Soil type	Well drained but moist in summer
Height	9 m/29 ft 6 in
Spread	9 m/29 ft 6 in
Propagation	From cuttings in a heated propagator in summer, or by layering in summer
Flowering period	Mid- to late summer

The star jasmine, *Trachelospermum jasminoides*, is a gentler, calmer and, if truth be told, classier, version of the true jasmine. This is an aristocratic plant that has everything going for it – glossy, dark green, evergreen leaves that turn slightly reddish in winter, and deliciously jasmine-scented flowers in summer. The flowers are small, white and star-shaped with a slight twist at the centre.

The problem with trachelospermum is the opposite to that of jasmine. Whereas jasmine races away and is almost impossible to contain, trachelospermum is slow to get going. It creeps along, taking several years to really get into its stride. But this is also one of its charms. You don't have to keep cutting it back, for a start. It will stay fairly neatly in a relatively small area, and pruning can be of the delicate snipping variety, rather than the panicked hacking type. But don't be too hasty with the pruning: you will get the best show of flowers if you can encourage the plant to grow upwards and then to cascade down. The flow of sap is restricted on stems that hang downwards, which discourages soft green growth and encourages harder, flowering wood to form.

In theory, trachelospermum is self-clinging, so you shouldn't need to provide support, but in reality its clinging powers are fairly weak. It definitely needs quite a lot of help to get started when first planted: tie the stems in loosely to a support. And if you want your more mature plants to cascade forwards without pulling themselves off the wall, you will certainly need to provide the support of a few wires or a sturdy trellis.

Trachelospermum's slow, steady nature also means that the growth has a pleasingly woody, mature character. The whole plant looks solid and well built – as if it's here to stay. It can be a little shy to flower, so the trick is to plant it in your sunniest spot. In fact, it is only frost-

hardy, so doesn't appreciate temperatures lower than –5°C/23°F. It really needs the warmth of a sunny south- or west-facing wall to grow well and won't thrive if it is subjected to cold winds.

To propagate, you can either take cuttings or layer the plant. Take 5–7½ cm/2–3 in cuttings in late summer. Remove the lower leaves, insert a few cuttings around the edge of a pot of gritty compost, then root them in a heated propagator. Layering involves taking a low-lying stem and pinning it to the ground with a tent peg or similar. Making a small nick on the underside of the stem where it touches the ground can help it to form roots. Once it has rooted, sever the rooted section from the plant and pot it on.

Wisteria floribunda

JAPANESE WISTERIA

Situation	Full sun or partial shade
Hardiness	Hardy (USDA zone 5)
Soil type	Moist but well drained
Height	9 m/29 ft 6 in
Spread	9 m/29 ft 6 in
Propagation	By layering in autumn
Flowering period	Early summer

Wisteria is always impressive. It romps away, twining its stems over its supports and, come early summer, it produces masses of racemes of 30 cm/12 in-long, pendent flowers. The effect is almost like a waterfall. As the stems mature, they very quickly take on a gnarled, characterful appearance that makes the plant look good even when it is not in leaf or flower.

Most wisterias, though not all, are scented, but *Wisteria floribunda* and its cultivars have a stronger scent at night and so make a wonderful addition to the night garden.

W. floribunda is also slightly less rampant than some other wisterias, but it's still a huge plant and needs a large support. You can grow it through a tree, which is how it grows in the wild, but to do this you will need to plant it away from the tree and leaning in towards it. To begin with, you may have to help it along with a bamboo cane or similar so that it can reach the tree. Once it does, you can tie it in to the tree, after which it should look after itself.

Wisteria looks wonderful trained against a house wall, but for this you will have to fix a series of parallel wires to the wall to act as support. (You can use a trellis, but it would have to be huge.) It is also the perfect plant for covering a well-built pergola; here the flowers will hang down completely unimpeded and will look their best.

Wisterias have a reputation for being slow to flower, so to avoid a long wait you need to take care when buying. Plants grown from seedlings can take up to 15 years to flower for the first time, but if you buy a plant that has been grafted onto a rootstock, it should flower in its first or second year. Ask when you buy, or look for the knobbly graft low down on the stem.

Soil next to walls can be very dry since the rain doesn't reach it, so if you are planting a wisteria against a wall, plant it as far away as

possible and lean it in towards the wall. Improve the soil before planting with garden compost or well-rotted farmyard manure. Plant in spring or autumn, then water well. If you are planting in spring, keep the wisteria well watered throughout summer. As it grows, train the shoots along the support.

Pruning is important to keep the plant within bounds and to encourage flowering. Ideally, pruning should be done twice a year, in late summer and in winter. In late summer, cut back any side shoots that aren't needed to extend the basic framework, leaving about six leaves on each shoot. In winter cut these back for a second time, leaving three buds.

Wisteria produces green seed pods in summer. Make sure children don't get hold of these, or any other parts of the plant, since they can cause extreme discomfort if eaten.

Zaluzianskya ovata

NIGHT PHLOX

Situation	Full sun
Hardiness	Frost-hardy (USDA zone 9)
Soil type	Moist but well drained
Height	25 cm/10 in
Spread	30 cm/12 in
Propagation	From cuttings in summer
Flowering period	Throughout summer

This low-growing, compact perennial from South Africa is a tiny, truly pretty plant that packs a huge punch scent-wise. It forms a dome of evergreen aromatic leaves and in midsummer is smothered in long, dark-red tubes topped with small deep-red buds. These open to reveal pale, pinkish-white inner petals, each one scalloped and gently cupped to reveal the strong contrast between the inner and the outer petals.

On summer mornings, the flowers start to open but, as the sun gets hot, they clamp shut again. It is only in the cool of the evening that they open fully and waft their spicy, sweet, complex honey-like aroma through the garden. It is very impressive for such a small plant and moths love it.

Zaluzianskya is half-hardy, which means it will tolerate a temperature of –5°C/23°F. In all but the mildest areas, you will have to grow it in a pot so it can be moved to a cool greenhouse or even a cold frame over winter. If you are planting it into the soil, it needs a rich, moist soil, but it must be well drained so the plant doesn't sit in water over winter. Mix in plenty of compost and grit when planting to try to achieve this tricky balance.

That's another reason why this plant works best in a pot: you can control the watering much more easily. It likes to be kept good and moist during the summer but fairly dry during winter, and that's hard to achieve when it is planted in the soil. Throughout summer, water frequently and feed once a week with a fertiliser that is high in flower-promoting potash, such as a tomato fertiliser or comfrey liquid.

These are short-lived perennials so they will gradually run out of steam and need replacing. They can also turn woody quickly if allowed to dry out in summer. If they do this, it's an indication that they are nearing the end of their useful lives. They generally stay fairly compact so you don't often have to cut back or prune, but it's a good idea to take cuttings each summer to ensure you always have young plants coming along as replacements. Take cuttings from non-flowering shoots and push them into pots of compost-and-vermiculite mix or compost-and-grit mix. It is a good idea to cover the pots with a clear plastic bag to keep them humid, and keep them cool and shady while the plants are taking root. Pot them on individually once they have rooted. You will need to overwinter these small plants carefully and plant them into larger pots for the patio the following spring, moving them outdoors when all chance of frost has passed.

SUPPORTING CAST

There are many beautiful, pale plants that aren't night-scented but that deserve a place in the night garden for their shape and purity of colour. I have included several white winter-flowering plants in this section, my idea being that you still need something to lure you out of the house and down the garden in the dead of winter. Some of these are beautifully scented, but not particularly so on chilly winter nights. Other important plants to consider for the night garden are those with silver leaves. Their metallic sheen reflects even low light; several are low-growing ground-cover plants that create rivers of night-shimmering silver among your other plants. I have also included a few particularly useful coloured plants. These will give your white garden a bit of colour and variety during the day, but will sink back into obscurity come evening.

Allium giganteum
ORNAMENTAL ALLIUM

Situation	Full sun
Hardiness	Hardy (USDA zone 8)
Soil type	Well drained
Height	1.5 m/5 ft
Spread	15 cm/6 in
Propagation	Lift bulbs in autumn and separate offsets to grow on
Flowering period	Summer

Ornamental onions are an essential ingredient in any cottage garden. The huge, purple, perfectly spherical flower heads of *Allium giganteum* float above the rest of the planting, providing an accent among the more mound-like shapes of many herbaceous perennials. Where they find conditions to their liking, they will multiply and gradually appear throughout your garden. Where the soil is too heavy, however, they will slowly peter out over a few years, and you will have to replant occasionally, just as you would with tulips.

Alliums like a well-drained soil and lots of sun in order to do well. Ideally, you should plant the bulbs in autumn, digging lots of grit into the area first. Don't be tempted just to line each planting hole with grit, however: in wet weather on heavier soils, the grit will simply act as a sump, drawing water from all around. You should plant your alliums at three times their own depth, so a bulb 7.5 cm/3 in across needs to be planted about 23 cm/9 in deep, with its pointed end upwards. They look best planted in groups. Either scatter them in a casually arranged clump or plant them in drifts through and between other plants. For the best flowers, you should feed them with a balanced fertiliser from the moment the leaves appear.

Anthemis punctata subsp. cupaniana

SICILIAN CHAMOMILE

Situation	Full sun
Hardiness	Hardy (USDA zone 5)
Soil type	Well drained
Height	30 cm/12 in
Spread	90 cm/36 in
Propagation	Sow seed in spring
Flowering period	Early to late summer

Sicilian chamomile is the perfect ground-cover or front-of-border plant for a moonlight garden. It has delicately cut silver foliage that creeps along the ground, forming a carpet that spills over the edges of paths, softening them gently. The leaves are at their most silver in summer and glint metallically on moonlit nights. In summer, this carpet of foliage is covered with a mass of small daisy-like flowers that keep their colour and freshness for a long time. In winter, the leaves turn greener but remain on the plant. The foliage is aromatic when crushed, which is another reason to use it by a path where it might occasionally be trodden on accidentally.

This is a plant for well-drained soils and looks good in a gravel garden. In heavier soils, mix plenty of grit around the planting hole when you plant. This chamomile will spread fairly quickly, but you can easily keep it neat. Trim the flowers off as soon as they fade to encourage a second flush, then trim again later on and a little harder to keep the plant small and bushy. The trimming will stimulate shoots lower down and so prevent legginess. Alternatively, you can leave the second flush of flowers to set seed, then the plant will seed itself freely around the garden.

Argyranthemum frutescens
MARGUERITE

Situation	Full sun
Hardiness	Half-hardy (USDA zone 10)
Soil type	Well drained
Height	60 cm/24 in
Spread	60 cm/24 in
Propagation	From cuttings in spring or summer
Flowering period	Early summer to early autumn

Marguerites are real powerhouses of summer-flower production. Often sold as bedding plants, they are far more sophisticated than your average blowsy, brightly coloured thing. They form a neat mound of bright green, finely cut leaves and produce big daisy-like flowers all summer long. You may also find them sold as standards or lollipops – balls of foliage on top of straight stems. A pair of these looks great either side of a door or pathway, their pure white flowers glowing in the dark. There are varieties that have very pretty yellow or pink flowers, but these won't show up so well at night.

Plant marguerites in well-drained soil or in containers in a mixture of grit and multi-purpose compost. They make useful bedding plants for seaside gardens as they are tolerant of salt and winds, but generally speaking they are not particularly hardy. In milder areas they may survive the winter, but you should cover their base with a thick mulch to protect them from the hardest frosts. In colder areas, you will need to overwinter them in an unheated greenhouse or a porch from autumn onwards. Plants that get frosted at the tips may grow back from their base in spring, but as a precaution against loss, take cuttings in summer and overwinter them carefully.

Choisya ternata
MEXICAN ORANGE BLOSSOM

Situation	Full sun
Hardiness	Hardy (USDA zone 8)
Soil type	Well drained
Height	2.5 m/8 ft
Spread	2.5 m/8 ft
Propagation	From cuttings in summer
Flowering period	Spring, summer and autumn

This luxuriously glossy-leaved, neat shrub would be worth growing just for its lustrous evergreen foliage, but in spring, and then later again in summer, it is covered in starry white flowers with a scent of orange blossom; hence the plant's common name. The scent isn't particularly strong at night, but the flowers look beautiful in the evening light and will scent your garden during the day. *Choisya ternata* 'Sundance' has glossy pale green, almost yellow leaves and the same flowers as the species. Both plants naturally form a compact, mounded shape.

These are hardy shrubs, but aren't actually the toughest, so they are best suited to gardens in milder areas or to sheltered, sunny corners in colder areas. Plant them in well-drained soil in full sun. Occasionally choisyas may be damaged by hard frosts. If this happens, you can prune them hard and they will produce a new flush of stems. Pruning back the flowered shoots by about 25 cm/10 in after the spring flush will keep the shrub bushy and dense and will encourage a later flush of flowers in summer and autumn.

These plants are good in a low-maintenance garden and, because they can put up with a degree of neglect, are a particularly good choice for a front garden.

Clematis montana
CLEMATIS

Situation	Full sun or partial shade (roots in shade)
Hardiness	Hardy (USDA zone 8)
Soil type	Fairly well drained
Height	7 m/23 ft
Spread	4 m/13 ft
Propagation	From cuttings in spring or early summer
Flowering period	Late spring

This is a huge, vigorous climber that you should plant only where it has space to romp away. But if you have a wall or an ugly outbuilding you want to cover, or a sturdy pergola over which to train it, and you can really let it grow furiously, clematis is a magnificent plant that is smothered in pale, scented flowers in late spring and into early summer. This mass of pale flowers makes a great backdrop for an evening planting scheme.

Clematis like sunshine but they don't like their roots to be hot, so either plant them where their feet are in the shade and their head is in the sun, or provide some ground-cover planting, such as hardy geraniums, around the base to keep them shaded. You will also need to provide sturdy supports for the plant to climb up. Stretched wires are good against a wall, or you can help them get started clambering up a pergola support by tying the stems in to begin with.

Always plant clematis a few centimetres/inches deeper than the level of the soil in the pot in which you bought it. They suffer from a fungal problem called clematis wilt, in which the stems can suddenly collapse and die. If you have planted your clematis deeply enough, you can simply cut the affected stems right down and more will sprout from below the ground.

Convallaria majalis
LILY OF THE VALLEY

Situation	Shade
Hardiness	Hardy (USDA zone 8)
Soil type	Moist, humus-rich
Height	25 cm/10 in
Spread	30 cm/12 in
Propagation	Dig up rhizomes in autumn, divide and replant
Flowering period	Late spring

Lily of the valley is a plant that signals the turning of the seasons from spring to summer. Its rich, sweet scent is well loved and, although it is not especially night-scented, its beautiful little dangling, bell-like flowers are pure white and will brighten up a gloomy corner early in the year. The leaves are wide and dark green and the racemes of white flowers tinted with green show up well against this background.

Lily of the valley isn't a dainty thing to be planted among other delicate spring beauties. Truth be told, it is a bit of a thug; you should plant it only where it has room to spread without bothering other plants.

Ideally, it wants a moist, humus-rich soil that mirrors that of its woodland habitat, so dig in plenty of leaf mould or garden compost before planting. An alternative is to grow it in pots for early flowers. Plant the 'pips' (as the small plants are called) in pots in spring and leave them in a greenhouse or cold frame. The extra heat and protection this affords forces them into early growth and flower. You can then treat them as temporary house plants and bring them indoors to enjoy their scent. Place them outside again as soon as the flowers have faded. If you are treating them this way, you will need to remove them from the pots, divide them and replant each year.

Digitalis purpurea f. albiflora
FOXGLOVE

Situation	Partial shade
Hardiness	Hardy (USDA zone 3)
Soil type	Humus-rich, well drained
Height	100 cm/40 in
Spread	50 cm/20 in
Propagation	Sow seeds in late spring and early summer
Flowering period	Late spring, early summer

Although they are not night-scented, white foxgloves send up impressive spires of white flowers that provide a strong vertical accent in an evening garden. *Digitalis purpurea* f. albiflora is pure white and – unlike many other foxgloves – the flowers are entirely unspotted and really glow in low-light conditions. Foxgloves are woodland plants, so they are most at home in dappled sun and well-drained but humus-rich soil. But they are pretty tolerant plants, so it is worth trying them in most soils.

Since these plants are biennials, sow seed in late spring or early summer for flowers the following year. Sow into seed trays filled with seed compost and prick the seedlings out into individual pots once they are large enough to handle. Plant them out in autumn where they are to flower. They die after flowering but self-seed readily, so once they are established you should never be left wanting. Leave the dead plants until spring to give them a chance to drop all their seed, then pull them up and compost them. One of the benefits of this self-seeding habit is that the spires pop up throughout the garden and you will find foxgloves in places you might not have thought to plant them. They look great in a cottage-garden border, but work just as well among ferns and other woodland plants.

All parts of foxgloves are highly poisonous, so take care to keep pets and children away from them.

Echinacea purpurea
PURPLE CONEFLOWER

Situation	Full sun or partial shade
Hardiness	Hardy (USDA zone 8)
Soil type	Humus-rich
Height	80 cm/30 in
Spread	30 cm/12 in
Propagation	From divisions in spring or autumn
Flowering period	Late summer

Echinaceas provide late-summer colour in perennial borders. While not really night plants – although there are pure white cultivars such as 'White Swan' that show up well in an evening planting – they are included here since they rub along very nicely with other cottage-garden perennials or in a mixed border. Plus, they will extend the season of interest in your garden into late summer and autumn, and even into winter. Once the petals have faded, the central cone stays on the plant a long time, providing a strong winter shape that is particularly pleasing after a hoar frost.

Echinaceas do well in most sunny or slightly shaded spots, but ideally they like a fertile soil and hate having permanently damp roots. To achieve this, mix organic matter and some grit into the soil when planting to ensure the soil is fertile and evenly moist but not too damp. They don't like having their roots disturbed, so only lift and divide after a good few years. Lift the plant in spring or autumn, shake the soil off, then use a sharp knife to divide the clump, ensuring each piece has some root and stem. Replant and keep well watered. They usually self-seed fairly freely so you shouldn't need to divide them purely for propagation, only to keep them healthy.

Galanthus nivalis
SNOWDROP

Situation	Partial shade
Hardiness	Hardy (USDA zone 8)
Soil type	Humus-rich
Height	10 cm/4 in
Spread	10 cm/4 in
Propagation	Lift and split clumps just after flowering
Flowering period	Winter

Chances are you won't be spending a great deal of time in the garden on mid- and late-winter nights, but it is good to have something to lure you out there. Otherwise, if you are out of the house all day, you are unlikely to see much of your garden at all during the winter months. A few pale-coloured winter plants may just tempt you away from the cosy fire and television for a few minutes. The ultimate pale-coloured winter plant just has to be the snowdrop.

Galanthus nivalis is the common snowdrop. You can buy them in their hundreds at a very reasonable price and scatter them throughout the garden. As they need constant moisture, they are best planted 'in the green' rather than as bulbs. When you buy bulbs, there is a risk that they will have dried out, which means they are likely to come up 'blind' – that is, they won't flower for at least the first year.

Use them en masse to create a carpet under deciduous shrubs and trees, or in little clumps among other plants. They are woodland plants and so prefer a moist, humus-rich soil and partial shade – the shade of trees is perfect. Planting time is just after flowering time.

Geranium pratense 'Mrs Kendall Clark'

GERANIUM

Situation	Full sun or partial shade
Hardiness	Hardy (USDA zone 8)
Soil type	Any
Height	90 cm/36 in
Spread	60 cm/24 in
Propagation	From divisions in spring or autumn
Flowering period	Early to midsummer, sometimes with a second flush

If you are looking for a dependable plant with masses of colourful flowers to accompany your pale night-bloomers, you could do worse than plant a hardy geranium. These low-growing, weed-smothering plants get covered in flowers in shades of purple, pink or white – ideal for complementing the pale, cool colours of a garden planted for the evening. Some have such pale flowers that they show up in the dark themselves; alternatively, you can use darker-flowered cultivars for a splash of daytime colour.

'Mrs Kendall Clark' falls somewhere between the two, as it has greyish-pink flowers with attractive white patterning. It blooms fairly early in the summer, but can be encouraged to produce a second flush if the whole plant is trimmed back by about a third just after the flowers have faded. For a more intense colour, choose *G.* 'Anne Folkard', which produces vibrant magenta flowers throughout summer and autumn. For a paler flower, consider *G.* 'Kashmir White', which produces white flowers with delicate pink veining all summer. If you trim these back after flowering, they will form a small, neat mound of leaves. Split plants in spring or autumn every few years to propagate them and to keep them healthy.

Helleborus niger

CHRISTMAS ROSE

Situation	Partial shade
Hardiness	Hardy (USDA zone 8)
Soil type	Moist, humus-rich
Height	30 cm/12 in
Spread	40 cm/15 in
Propagation	From divisions or sow seed in spring
Flowering period	Winter to early spring

Most winter flowers are tiny little things that have taken the evolutionary path of going small to avoid the ravages of winter weather. Hellebores have instead opted to go tough. Their flowers are the biggest of all the winter blooms: they really are quite an impressive size for a winter flower, and that's because their petals (technically 'sepals') are solid and weather-resistant. *Helleborus niger*, the Christmas rose, has pure white petals. Its flowers aren't as pendent (drooping) as some hellebores, which helps them to show up on a dark winter night. They are a great choice for a front garden, where they will greet you cheerily as you get home on cold, dark evenings. This is an evergreen plant and so bears its dark, glossy leaves (all the better to show up the flowers) year-round.

Hellebores are useful plants because they thrive in shade. Ideally the shade should be of the dappled, woodland variety, but they are not hugely fussy. They like a moist, humus-rich soil, so dig in lots of leaf mould or garden compost before planting. You should also spread a thick mulch of leaf mould or compost over the soil every autumn. This not only enriches the soil, but also provides a background that shows the plant off to best advantage when it flowers.

Hydrangea arborescens 'Annabelle'

HYDRANGEA

Situation	Sun or partial shade
Hardiness	Hardy (USDA zone 8)
Soil type	Moist, humus-rich, but well drained
Height	2 m/6 ft 6 in
Spread	2 m/6 ft 6 in
Propagation	From cuttings in summer
Flowering period	Early summer to early autumn

Hydrangeas have a reputation for being slightly naff and suburban, but they are wonderfully dependable, fuss-free plants that produce masses of huge flowers throughout summer. Personally, I love the coloured ones, but if you are a bit squeamish about having them in your garden, you should still consider making room for 'Annabelle'. It is an extremely classy plant that even the most fashion-conscious gardener couldn't turn their nose up at. It produces small green globes of buds that turn into huge, pure-white footballs – great for looming out from the far reaches of your night garden. In autumn, these become architectural seed heads that stay on the plant all winter and glisten in the frost.

These are easy, hardy plants that don't take a great deal of looking after once they are established. Plant them in spring or autumn in a sunny or partially shaded spot, water them until they are established – and that's it. These plants will survive drought (although they produce smaller flowers in drier soils) and aren't bothered by cold. Each spring, remove the tips of the stems back to the first shooting bud and remove any dead stems right back to their base. Apart from that, a hydrangea shouldn't need much in the way of pruning unless it gets too large. If that happens, cut back about a third of the oldest stems each spring, right back to their base.

Lavandula angustifolia 'Hidcote'
LAVENDER

Situation	Full sun
Hardiness	Hardy (USDA zone 8)
Soil type	Well drained
Height	60 cm/24 in
Spread	70 cm/27 in
Propagation	From cuttings in summer
Flowering period	Mid- to late summer

Lavender has reflective silvery foliage but also produces spikes of flowers in shades ranging from pure white to deepest purple, so it is a great plant either for creating or for complementing an evening planting scheme. *Lavandula angustifolia* 'Hidcote' is a compact lavender often used for hedging because of its ability to keep a good shape. It has particularly pale foliage and contrasting deep purple flowers. Both foliage and flowers are, famously, scented, especially so when they release their volatile oils in the heat of the day. The scent continues a little into the evening, too, particularly when the plants are handled.

Lavenders suit Mediterranean plantings, but also work well as an understorey for roses and other shrubs. They look good in a gravel garden and do well by the sea. They make the perfect edging plant for paths, particularly as they will release their oils when brushed against.

You can treat lavenders in one of two ways: either let them grow all summer and flower in mid- to late summer, then trim them lightly all over; or trim them every now and then all summer to prevent them flowering and to create a piece of lavender topiary. This makes for an unusual and impressive effect. Never prune lavenders back hard and be aware that they are fairly short-lived plants and will eventually need replacing.

Lonicera fragrantissima
WINTER HONEYSUCKLE

Situation	Full sun or partial shade
Hardiness	Hardy (USDA zone 8)
Soil type	Humus-rich
Height	2 m/6 ft 6 in
Spread	2.5 m/8 ft
Propagation	From cuttings in summer
Flowering period	Late winter to early spring

Many winter-flowering shrubs are scented, although not especially night-scented. There are few night-flying insects around on winter nights and it is pretty hard work attracting any pollinators in the depths of winter without becoming a specialist gardener. But shrubs such as Hamamelis, *Viburnum x bodnantense* and *Lonicera fragrantissima* are worth growing for their daytime scent, while *L. fragrantissima* is also useful for the evening garden. Its arching sprays of pink-tinged white flowers will stand out on dark winter nights and may even tempt you down to the far reaches of the garden to catch a waft of their spring-like lemony scent.

This plant is a shrubby honeysuckle and has little in common, habit-wise, with the climbing honeysuckle. It does, however, share that plant's ability to produce a wonderful fragrance. It will grow in sun or partial shade, but you will get a better display of flowers if it is grown in full sun. Plant in evenly moist but not wet soil that has been enriched with plenty of organic matter. Pruning to keep it within bounds always makes this plant look a little awkward, so try to plant it where it will have plenty of room to spread out. If the branches become congested, remove up to a third of them each year, right back to their base.

Paeonia 'Claire de Lune'
PEONY

Situation	Full sun or partial shade
Hardiness	Hardy (USDA zone 7)
Soil type	Rich, moist and fertile but well drained
Height	80 cm/30 in
Spread	70 cm/27 in
Propagation	From divisions in autumn or early spring
Flowering period	Late spring to midsummer

Peonies defy rational gardening logic. They flower for an extremely brief spell, making a glorious statement in the garden for a short while, and look fairly dull for the rest of the year. But what flowers they produce! They are always big and impressively luxurious, and they are always a talking point. Peonies are one of those flowers that you just have to take a deep breath and plant – the horticultural equivalent of buying yourself the occasional expensive pair of shoes.

They are hungry plants, and won't tolerate mean conditions, so you should plant them in a really humus-rich soil that retains moisture well yet allows excess water to drain away. Mulch thickly with well-rotted manure or garden compost once a year to ensure the soil stays rich. Remove dead flowers after they have faded and remove any foliage that looks spotted: this is the first signs of botrytis.

'Claire de Lune' has an unusual flower. It is huge, single and with sweet-scented pale yellow petals, but the centre is made up of a great many golden yellow stamens, so it looks like a fluffy golden ball. The flowers show up well in moonlight (hence the name), but if you can't find this cultivar, there are many other pale yellow, pale pink and white-flowered peonies to choose from, many of them scented.

Philadelphus 'Beauclerk'
MOCK ORANGE

Situation	Full sun or partial shade
Hardiness	Hardy (USDA zone 8)
Soil type	Fairly well drained
Height	2.5 m/8 ft
Spread	2.5 m/8 ft
Propagation	From cuttings in summer, autumn or winter
Flowering period	Midsummer

Philadelphus is a shrub that has all the exuberance of summer. It blooms once a year in midsummer and pretty briefly, it must be admitted, but the flowers are large, white and fragrant. They are not especially night-scented – the plant's aim is to attract day-flying pollinators rather than night-flying ones – but they bring a strong orange-blossom scent to the garden by day, and by night they positively glow.

Philadelphus 'Beauclerk' has an arching habit that produces a fountain of impressive white flowers with slightly pink-flushed centres. To make the most of the fountain-like effect, plant it in a spot where it will have plenty of room to shoot out its flower sprays, otherwise the effect will be ruined. Pruning is simple; after it has finished flowering, cut about a third of the oldest stems out completely, right down to the ground.

You may question whether it is worth making space for a shrub that flowers so briefly, but you can extend its season of interest by growing a climber through it, such as a small clematis. It looks good in a shrub border or at the back of a cottage-garden border. There are many cultivars to choose from, including the compact *P.* 'Manteau de Hermine' and the yellow-leaved *P. coronarius* 'Aureus'.

Rosa 'Madame Hardy'; *Rosa* 'Iceberg'

ROSE

Situation	Full sun
Hardiness	Hardy (USDA zone 3)
Soil type	Humus-rich
Height	2 m/6 ft 6 in
Spread	1 m/3 ft 3 in
Propagation	From cuttings in spring or autumn
Flowering period	Early to late summer

Roses are no more scented in the evening than they are in the day, but they do add an additional gentle scent to the garden at night, and a floriferous white rose, covering a fence or wall, is a glorious sight in the evening.

'Madame Hardy' is a damask rose and an old French variety. This is the one to go for if you want a short-lived blast of strong, delicious scent in early summer at the height of the rose season. 'Iceberg' blooms throughout the summer and into early autumn, but the scent isn't quite so magnificent. The choice is yours – or perhaps you have room in your garden for both.

Roses love a really rich soil and do particularly well in clay that has been improved with plenty of well-rotted horse manure or garden compost. You can grow them in sandier soils, too, but they are never quite so good. Whatever the soil, mulch regularly once a year. Feed regularly from early spring onwards with a high-potash fertiliser, such as tomato feed, to encourage flowering.

Climbers need to be carefully trained and pruned if they are not to shoot straight to the top of the support and flower only where passing birds can enjoy them. Provide a sturdy trellis or series of wires to support them. Try to tie the shoots into as horizontal a position as you can to encourage more flowers. Do this when pruning, and again throughout summer as long, whippy growths appear. Prune in autumn or winter, removing the oldest stems completely and reducing side shoots that have flowered by two-thirds.

Rosmarinus officinalis
ROSEMARY

Situation	Full sun
Hardiness	Hardy (USDA zone 8)
Soil type	Well drained
Height	1.5 m/5 ft
Spread	1.5 cm/1/2 in
Propagation	From cuttings in summer
Flowering period	Early spring to midsummer

Rosemary is an aromatic Mediterranean shrub with greyish-green, slightly silvery leaves. It makes a good background plant for a scheme of other silver-leaved Mediterranean plants and also looks good among herbaceous perennials. It is evergreen and therefore looks good all winter when other plants have died back or lost their leaves. It also produces purple-blue flowers over an extremely long period, starting early in spring. This makes it a useful plant for wildlife, providing nectar for early-flying bees and other insects at a time when supplies are low.

Treat rosemary as you would any other silver-leaved Mediterranean plant: it wants a well-drained soil and plenty of sun. If the soil is too rich, it is likely to become leggy, and in damp soils there may be some rotting off. But it is a little more tolerant and hardier than many other silver-leaved plants.

Like all silver-leaved plants, rosemary is likely to die if you cut it back hard, but it does get leggy with age. You can put this off for a while by trimming it back lightly into the young growth every year after the first flush of flowers has faded. However, it's generally considered short-lived. After a few years, it will start to show its age, becoming woody and gappy. There's not much you can do then but replace it.

Salvia officinalis 'Tricolor'
SAGE

Situation	Full sun or very light shade
Hardiness	Hardy (USDA zone 8)
Soil type	Well drained
Height	1 m/3 ft 3 in
Spread	1 m/3 ft 3 in
Propagation	From cuttings in spring or early summer
Flowering period	Early summer

Salvia officinalis 'Tricolor' is a very pretty, aromatic Mediterranean herb. It has greyish-green foliage edged in cream and the tips of the growths are tinged with purple. I have included sage as a night-garden plant because the variegation of the leaves helps it to show up in the dark.

Hailing from the Mediterranean, sage needs well-drained soil and sun, although it can take a little light shade.

In summer, sage will produce spikes of lilac-blue flowers; you will get a better-shaped plant and nicer leaves if you prevent it from flowering by regularly nipping out the top few leaves. This keeps the plant bushy and produces lots of fresh purple-flushed new leaves. Sage, along with other silver-leaved plants, doesn't take kindly to being pruned hard, so this constant nipping out is essential to keep the plant in good shape.

These plants are usually grown for their aromatic foliage. You can use it in cooking – in traditional stuffings, in pork or chicken recipes and in sage oils for pasta dishes – just like the plain-leaved sage.

Sage plants are short-lived sub-shrubs and will need replacing after five or six years.

Santolina chamaecyparissus
COTTON LAVENDER

Situation	Full sun
Hardiness	Frost-hardy (USDA zone 10)
Soil type	Well drained
Height	50 cm/20 in
Spread	90 cm/36 in
Propagation	From cuttings in summer
Flowering period	Mid- to late summer

Cotton lavender, the common name for *Santolina chamaecyparissus*, grows into a neat, dome-like mound of greyish-green foliage topped with hundreds of little button-like flowers on long stalks. It is an extremely neat plant with a pleasing habit and shape, and it will add an unusual texture to a planting scheme of Mediterranean plants. The pale yellow flowers show up well in the dark, as do the slightly silvery leaves and stems. The aromatic foliage produces its strongest scent during the heat of the day, but it continues to exude scent into the evening and is particularly noticeable if you are passing close by.

The trick is to plant cotton lavender in well-drained soil in full sun. In shadier spots, it is likely to become leggy; in damp soil it may rot. Ordinary garden soil is perfectly adequate: anything richer can lead to leggy growth and disease. Just work in plenty of grit before planting. You can treat this purely as a foliage plant – almost as a piece of topiary – by trimming it back frequently throughout the year to keep a really neat shape and discourage flowering. Alternatively, trim back into the current year's growth after the flowers have faded. In winter, protect the stems with a thick mulch.

Stachys byzantina 'Silver Carpet'

LAMB'S EAR

Situation	Full sun
Hardiness	Hardy (USDA zone 8)
Soil type	Well drained
Height	40 cm/15 in
Spread	60 cm/24 in
Propagation	Dig up, sever and pot on rooted stems in spring
Flowering period	Non-flowering (flowering varieties flower early summer to autumn)

Stachys is a ground-cover plant that is great for providing weed-suppressing growth along the front of a border. 'Silver Carpet', with its particularly felty silvery leaves, lives up to its name. The silvery effect is created by thousands of tiny, silky white hairs that cover the leaves. The species is native to Turkey and Iran; the purpose of these hairs is to deflect sunlight in these hot climates, but this reflective quality works equally well in moonlight. 'Silver Carpet' is a non-flowering cultivar, so all of its energy goes into producing its incredibly soft, tactile foliage. Grow it among your white, night-scented flowers to provide a silvery background.

All silver-leaved plants prefer a well-drained soil and this one is no exception. If your soil is not naturally sandy or light, mix plenty of grit in and around the planting hole. You should also choose a sunny spot. Thanks to its preference for well-drained soil and its silvery sheen, stachys will look entirely at home in a gravel garden, but it works equally well as an edging plant in a cottage-garden border. You will need to keep the ground around and between the stems weed-free while the plant is getting established, but once it has formed a good, thick mat, it should prevent weeds from germinating.

Tanacetum ptarmiciflorum

SILVER FEATHER

Situation	Full sun
Hardiness	Half-hardy (USDA zone 11)
Soil type	Well drained, sandy
Height	50 cm/20 in
Spread	40 cm/15 in
Propagation	Sow seeds in early spring or take cuttings in summer
Flowering period	Late summer

The extreme silver, almost white, finely cut feather-like leaves of *Tanacetum ptarmiciflorum* make it shine out in low light. But this is not a very hardy plant and is most often grown as an annual foliage filler for bedding schemes. In hanging baskets and containers it makes the perfect foil for white flowers. For moonlight garden bedding, team it with white petunias and you will have a magically pale, silvery scheme that is also night-scented.

These plants like well-drained compost and will tolerate a little drought – a trait that makes them even better candidates for hanging baskets or pots, as these often get neglected at some point over the summer. When you are planting them, mix some grit or vermiculite into the compost for good drainage.

They do produce yellow flowers later in the summer, but the trick is not to let them flower. Pinch out the tips occasionally throughout the summer and you will keep the plant small and bushy and force it to produce young, fresh-looking growth instead of growing large and leggy.

It is a little tricky to keep these plants going from year to year, but you can take cuttings in summer and overwinter them in a cool greenhouse. Otherwise, grow from seed in early spring or buy small plants in mid-spring.

Tulipa 'White Triumphator'
TULIP

Situation	Full sun
Hardiness	Hardy (USDA zone 8)
Soil type	Well drained
Height	60 cm/24 in
Spread	15 cm/6 in
Propagation	Lift bulbs in summer and separate offsets to grow on
Flowering period	Late spring

Tulips appear at a time when the evenings are getting lighter and warmer and you may just be starting to spend a little extra time outside, pottering around weeding and getting your garden in order for the summer days to come. 'White Triumphator' is a particularly elegant tulip, tall and stately with pure white, curved petals. A few groups of these around your garden on a warm, late spring evening will be sure to lure you out of the house with a glass of wine in your hand.

There are only very few situations where you can throw tulips in the ground and depend on them to come back year after year. They like really well-drained soil and a sunny position, so if you can provide a spot where they are guaranteed to get a baking each summer and not sit in damp soil through the winter, they may last quite a long time.

In such spots, be sure to plant them extra deep. Plant them in late autumn, as this helps to keep them going. On heavier soils, they will simply fade away and the flowering will be greatly reduced even in the second year from planting.

Many people lift their tulips after the leaves have faded, store them somewhere dry for the winter, then replant them in autumn. Others simply buy fresh bulbs each year. This is really the only way to guarantee a great display, but it is rather extravagant.

Verbena bonariensis

VERBENA

Situation	Full sun
Hardiness	Frost-hardy (USDA zone 8)
Soil type	Moist but well drained
Height	1.5 m/5 ft
Spread	45 cm/18 in
Propagation	Sow seed in autumn or spring
Flowering period	Midsummer to autumn

Verbena bonariensis is a plant that drifts through other plantings. It has tall, wiry stems topped with little heads of small purple flowers. One of the pleasures of this plant is that it is almost transparent so you can plant it anywhere in a border – even at the front – without blocking out the view of the plants behind. It will self-seed freely if it likes the conditions, so you will end up with plants all through your borders as well as popping up in cracks in patios and paths.

Verbena is a perfectly lovely purple in the daytime and will blend in with all manner of colour schemes, from hot and fiery to cool and pastel. I have included it here because of what it does in the evening. Just as other purple flowers start to fade into the gloom, the flowers of *V. bonariensis* begin to glow. It is almost as if a little light has been switched on inside each one, providing pinpricks of bright purple scattered throughout the garden. They are quite a sight. Of course, they eventually disappear into the darkness and only the true whites remain, glowing away, but this verbena more than earns its keep in the early evening garden.

In some areas, this verbena can prove slightly tender, so you should cover the crowns with a thick mulch over winter. You will usually have enough new seedlings scattered about, however, to make up for any winter losses.

Zantedeschia aethiopica
TRUMPET LILY

Situation	Full sun
Hardiness	Frost-hardy (USDA zone 9)
Soil type	Moist or as a marginal aquatic
Height	90 cm/36 in
Spread	50 cm/20 in
Propagation	From divisions in spring
Flowering period	Late spring to midsummer

It is not just average back gardens that can be turned into twilight gardens. You can also plant up a pond or a bog garden for evening viewing. The moisture-loving herbaceous perennial *Zantedeschia aethiopica* produces fabulous large pure-white spathes – petal-like structures wrapped around the true flowers, which are borne in a spike or 'spadex'. Imagine them appearing to float serenely above a moonlit pond or gently lit from below by a few floating candles. And, when the plant isn't in flower, it has attractive glossy green arrow-shaped leaves, too.

Ideally, this plant needs really damp soil, like that in a bog garden, but you can try growing it in normal garden soil enriched with lots of organic matter such as well-rotted horse manure or garden compost. It is only frost-hardy so can't tolerate temperatures below –5°C/23°F. In most areas, once the plants have died back, it is a good idea to protect them over winter by applying a thick mulch of bark chippings or similar. They can also be grown as marginal plants in a pond, but will need lifting out over winter.

To propagate them, lift the clump in spring or autumn and split it using a fork or spade. Replant immediately and keep well watered. 'Crowborough' is a cultivar with particularly large white spathes and architectural leaves.

BACKSTAGE BEAUTIES

Not all your plants need to be showy and glitzy. Some have to do the hard work, providing the garden with backbone and solidity. These are the trees, shrubs and hedges. You might use some of these plants in any garden, but there are certain backbone plants that are particularly good at night. Some are silvery or white, such as the silver birch or the weeping pear, both of which will glint away in even the lowest of light. Others, such as yew, are particularly dense and dark. They are ideal for throwing the whites and pales into sharp relief.

Hedging plants are particularly important in evening gardens. They filter wind and help create an enclosed, sheltered space that slows the movement of air and keeps night-time scents trapped close by. Some hedging plants also work extremely well as topiary, which can be interspersed among your pale, ephemeral beauties to provide strong structural effects. I have also included several plants here for their dramatic or craggy silhouettes, which will provide an arresting outline against the night sky.

Abies koreana

KOREAN FIR

Situation	Full sun or partial shade
Hardiness	Hardy (USDA zone 8)
Soil type	Moist, well drained, slightly acidic
Height	6 m/19 ft 6 in
Spread	3 m/9 ft 9 in
Propagation	Sow seed in autumn
Flowering period	Cones in late spring

Most conifers either grow too large for the average garden or stay squat and tiny and just look silly. *Abies koreana* finds the happy middle ground between the two. It grows extremely slowly, but has a strong presence and stature, and could certainly not be called a dwarf conifer. It earns its place in the evening garden partly because of its excellent silhouette but also thanks to its needles. These are bright green on top with silver undersides. Because of their upward-pointing habit, the undersides are most beautifully revealed, giving the whole plant a silvery-blue sheen. The cultivar 'Silberlocke' has curved, slightly twisted needles that reveal the whole of their underside. This makes the plant even more silvery and even better suited to a moonlit garden.

In spring and into early summer, impressive violet-blue, upward-pointing cones are produced all over the branches. These hold fast all through the year, gradually turning brown as autumn approaches.

This is a spreading tree that really can't be pruned to fit a space. Any attempt at pruning it will make it look extremely awkward, so choose a spot where it can spread out and achieve its full, majestic form. Ideally, you should plant it in full sun, but it can take some shade.

Amelanchier lamarckii
SNOWY MESPILUS, JUNE BERRY

Situation	Full sun or partial shade
Hardiness	Hardy (USDA zone 8)
Soil type	Acid, moist, well drained
Height	6 m/19 ft 6 in
Spread	3 m/9 ft 9 in
Propagation	Sow seed in autumn
Flowering period	Spring

While the pinnacle of evening sitting-out time is obviously the summer, when the breezes are warm and night-scented plants are in full flood, it is good to have palely visible plants in the garden at other times of the year, too. Amelanchier is a beautiful white-flowered plant for early spring. It becomes so smothered in white flowers that it has the rather lovely common name of snowy mespilus. This is a plant that works hard for its place in the garden for most of the year, which makes it the perfect choice for a small garden. In spring there's that mass of white flowers; in summer it forms red, edible berries; and in autumn the foliage turns an impressive orange and red. In winter the plant isn't quite so spectacular, but it does have smooth, tactile, grey bark that looks good when the leaves have fallen.

The berries (hence its other common name, June berry) are edible, tasty, juicy and fruity with a hint of almond. Unfortunately, birds love them, too, so you'll need to net the tree if you want to be sure of getting them before the birds. If this is too much trouble, just be philosophical about it and view the berries as a boon for your birds.

Amelanchier prefers a moist, acid soil, but will tolerate a little dryness once it is really well established. It makes a small tree or a large, multi-stemmed shrub.

Betula utilis var. jacquemontii

HIMALAYAN BIRCH

Situation	Full sun or dappled shade
Hardiness	Hardy (USDA zone 8)
Soil type	Moist, well drained
Height	Up to 18 m/59 ft
Spread	Up to 9 m/29 ft 6 in
Propagation	From grafts in winter
Flowering period	Catkins in spring

Silver birch has pure white stems that provide a ghostly outline in the night garden. A group of several of them is an impressive sight, particularly if they are planted close together. They look good in winter, when the leaves have fallen and the bark is revealed in all its glory. They are also great for providing a truly dramatic backdrop to a garden planted for an evening use.

Betula utilis var. jacquemontii, the Himalayan birch, has even whiter bark than silver birch. It is the most popular and widely available of the really white-stemmed birches, but others are even whiter. *B. u.* var. jacquemontii 'Grayswood Ghost' has possibly the palest bark of all. Over time, the bark will start to get a little dull. Sometimes the outer layers peel off, revealing fresh white bark beneath, but you can help it along by giving it a bit of a scrub with slightly soapy water. This is a particularly good idea come winter, when you really want the bark to gleam.

Make sure you choose a tree that isn't going to outgrow the available space. Silver birches look terrible when pruned; they really need to be left just to grow. If your space is restricted, look for a smaller-growing cultivar such as *B. u.* var. jacquemontii 'Moonbeam'.

Buxus sempervirens

BOX

Situation	Partial shade (ideally) or full sun
Hardiness	Hardy (USDA zone 8)
Soil type	Moist, well drained
Height	Up to 5 m/16 ft 4 in if left unpruned (usually grown as a hedge or topiary)
Spread	Up to 5 m/16 ft 4 in if left unpruned
Propagation	From cuttings in summer
Flowering period	Can produce small flowers in spring

Box is a wonderfully malleable plant. It can be shaped into any form you can imagine, from teacups to peacocks to flying saucers. It makes a pretty nifty small hedge for edging a border, but it can also be allowed to grow far larger – to make a full-sized hedge as a backdrop to an evening border if you wish. Admittedly, it isn't as dark as yew, but its small round leaves are very textural and it becomes particularly dense and attractive if it is clipped regularly. You just can't help running your hands over a well-maintained box ball. Box topiary among flowering plants will anchor the scheme and provide structure that lasts all winter long. In spring it is covered in beautifully fresh, lime-green shoots.

Although box will survive in most conditions, it is really at its most glowing, emerald best in part-shade, which makes it a great choice for shadier spots. In full sun, the leaves can become a bit red and bleached, particularly if the roots are dry. Trim into shape once a year in early summer and repeat in late summer for a really crisp finish that will last through winter.

Carpinus betulus

HORNBEAM

Situation	Full sun or partial shade
Hardiness	Hardy (USDA zone 8)
Soil type	Fairly well drained
Height	23 m/75 ft if left unpruned
Spread	18 m/59 ft if left unpruned
Propagation	Sow seed in autumn
Flowering period	Catkins in spring

Hornbeam is a wonderful hedging plant for a night-time garden. It provides privacy and creates a sheltered environment where scents can linger long into the evening. It has similar-sized and shaped leaves to beech and, like beech, it is deciduous and will cling onto its leaves over winter if it is trimmed back regularly. The spring leaves are a pale, yellowy green; the summer leaves are mid-green; and the winter leaves are mid-brown, unlike the flashy glowing copper of winter beech leaves. Hornbeam's leaves are still very attractive – just subtler.

Hornbeam is a better choice than beech in moister, heavier soils. It will also stand much colder conditions than beech, so it is the best choice if you are planting in a frost pocket. Make a trench the length of your hedge and mix in lots of organic matter before backfilling. Plant bare-rooted plants in winter, spacing them 45 cm/18 in apart. For a really thick, dense hedge, plant a second, staggered row about 40 cm/15 in behind the first. Hornbeam is also worth considering as a pleached hedge. This is essentially a 'hedge on stilts'; it is a great way of creating a formal structure that can be underplanted with more informal planting. Prune in late summer for the best leaf retention through winter.

Cercis canadensis 'Forest Pansy'
REDBUD

Situation	Full sun or partial shade
Hardiness	Hardy (USDA zone 8)
Soil type	Fairly moist with good drainage
Height	9 m/29 ft 6 in
Spread	9 m/29 ft 6 in
Propagation	By layering in spring or from cuttings in summer
Flowering period	Spring

This deep purple-leaved tree is a real beauty. It is yet another plant for adding depth of colour to a white scheme or simply for providing a dark background against which to show off a white scheme at its best. In spring, before the leaves come out, it produces purple or pink pea-like flowers. On a mature plant these can make an impressive show, but the plant's main feature is its heart-shaped leaves, which taper off into elegant, slender tips. They are darkest purple and glossy when they emerge, and turn a slightly duller reddish-green in summer. They then make up for this dullness by becoming a myriad of reds and golden yellows in autumn, often from the inside of the tree outwards, which creates the impression that the tree is being lit up from within.

Planting one of these small, multi-stemmed trees is perhaps the best way of getting really spectacular autumn foliage into a small garden. They look a little awkward as youngsters, but over the years they slowly grow into themselves. You can plant them against a wall or at the back of a border, but they look particularly good planted where they will have the autumn evening sun behind them. Then the coloured leaves light up like stained glass. Quite amazing!

Cordyline australis
CABBAGE PALM

Situation	Full sun
Hardiness	Frost-hardy (USDA zone 10)
Soil type	Well drained
Height	5 m/16 ft 4 in
Spread	3 m/9 ft 9 in
Propagation	Sow seeds in spring or remove and pot up suckers in spring
Flowering period	Summer

Cordyline cuts quite a dash if the climate is mild enough for it to grow large. It forms a central stem from which emanate arching, strap-like leaves with pointed ends. When it is small, cordyline can be used as a centrepiece for a bedding arrangement or can simply be planted in a pot. In milder areas, you can try planting it in a border and seeing how it fares, but choose the plain green species as this is hardier than the variegated or red-leaved cultivars. If conditions permit, it can grow into a large, substantial plant with a spectacularly spiky silhouette; if it's happy, it will send out branches. I have included it here because it makes such a wonderful silhouette plant for the back of a night-time border.

In colder areas, you may have to keep it in a pot and move it into a cold greenhouse or porch each winter. Alternatively, try leaving it outdoors and protecting it with a swathe of horticultural fleece over the winter. Even in milder areas, the leaves can get battered by winds. Some people tie the leaves together to stop this from happening, but this looks quite ugly and isn't really necessary.

Cotinus coggygria 'Royal Purple'
SMOKE BUSH

Situation	Full sun or partial shade
Hardiness	Hardy (USDA zone 8)
Soil type	Fairly moist with good drainage
Height	4 m/13 ft
Spread	4 m/13 ft
Propagation	By layering in spring or from cuttings in summer
Flowering period	Late summer

Cotinus coggygria 'Royal Purple' may seem a brooding shrub, but it is extremely useful. Its round leaves are dark purple and provide the perfect foil for all sorts of different-coloured flowers. They tone well with deep red roses and purple verbenas, making the colours of these look richer and deeper. They also provide a strong contrast to pale colours and acid greens. A pale pastel or white evening planting needs a darker accent in its midst to give it a bit of backbone, and cotinus is the perfect plant for this.

Cotinus is an extremely common shrub, so it's easy to think of it as not very special, but in fact it possesses some wonderful subtleties. When the leaves first emerge, they have a silky grey sheen; when they open, their midribs are a vibrant pink that sparks the purple foliage into life and prevents it becoming too sombre. In autumn, the leaves turn scarlet and pink before they fall.

Cotinus is often commonly known as the smoke bush because of its haze of flowers produced in late summer. If you want these, you should let the plant grow naturally, only pruning the oldest wood lightly. But if you want the largest, most impressive foliage, you should prune established plants right to the ground each spring.

Fagus sylvatica

BEECH

Situation	Full sun or partial shade
Hardiness	Hardy (USDA zone 8)
Soil type	Well drained
Height	23 m/75 ft if left unpruned
Spread	18 m/59 ft if left unpruned
Propagation	Sow seed in autumn
Flowering period	Spring

Beech makes a wonderful hedge. It is not particularly dark or dense, unlike evergreen box or yew, but it has a charm of its own. You should definitely consider it as a backdrop to a night-time border, particularly where the soil is sandy.

Beech has fairly large leaves compared to box and yew, and isn't evergreen. But the beauty of beech is that its leaves turn a gorgeous coppery colour in autumn, then cling to the plant all winter, so you get the privacy and all-year-round cover of an evergreen as well as seasonal change. The leaves finally fall in spring as the fresh green folds of the new leaves appear all over the hedge.

Beech does like well-drained soil, so don't try to plant it anywhere remotely boggy. This makes it a particularly useful hedging plant for dryer areas and anywhere affected by drought. Dig out a trench the length of the hedge and backfill with a mixture of organic matter and soil before planting. To make sure the beech gets well established, it is best to plant bare-rooted plants in winter.

Trimming the hedge regularly to keep it relatively small helps it retain its leaves over winter. To achieve the best leaf retention, trim in fairly late summer.

Laurus nobilis

BAY

Situation	Full sun or partial shade
Hardiness	Frost-hardy (USDA zone 10)
Soil type	Fairly moist with good drainage
Height	12 m/39 ft 4 in
Spread	9 m/29 ft 6 in
Propagation	Sow seed in autumn or take cuttings in summer
Flowering period	Spring

Left unpruned, bay can make a huge evergreen plant and could even be considered a pretty good backdrop for a pale planting, but it is more often shaped into topiary and most often into a lollipop – a sphere of foliage balanced on top of a straight stem. In this guise, bay can provide a point of structure and solidity among floatier, paler, night-scented flowers.

You can buy bay trees ready-trained or you can train your own. If you are training your own, look for a young plant with a straight stem. If you can't find one, cut all the growth back in early spring to encourage a flush of fresh, straight stems, then you can select the most promising and cut the rest right back to the ground. Push a bamboo cane into the soil close to the stem and tie the stem to it as it grows. When it has reached the desired height for the top of your lollipop, nip out the tip. Branches will start to grow from just below this point. You should also completely remove any side shoots that emerge from the main stem. It will take a few years, but gradually the lollipop head will fill out and the plant can take its place in the garden.

Malus domestica
APPLE TREE

Situation	Full sun
Hardiness	Hardy (USDA zone 8)
Soil type	Moist, well drained
Height	From 1 m/3 ft 3 in to 4 m/13 ft, depending on rootstock
Spread	1 m/3 ft 3 in to 4.5 m/14 ft 9 in, depending on rootstock
Propagation	From bud grafts in winter
Flowering period	Spring
Fruiting period	Late summer to autumn

Every garden should contain a fruit tree or two. Apple trees have wonderfully craggy outlines and a large specimen can create a fine silhouette against the night sky or at the back of a border. If you have a small garden, choose a smaller variety: it will still lend a garden maturity within a very few years. In spring, just as the evenings are getting lighter, the trees are covered in beautiful white and pink blossom. There are few more reliable crops than apples and, come late summer and autumn, a mature tree will produce armfuls of fruit.

Choosing the correct-sized plant for your garden is easy since apple trees are grafted onto a number of different rootstocks. The rootstock determines the rate of growth. M27 is the tiniest and the one to choose for pots, growing to just 1 m/3 ft 3 in by 1 m/3 ft 3 in. M9 reaches 1.9 m/6 ft 3 in by 1.9 m/6 ft 3 in; M26 1.8 m/5 ft 10 in by 2.3 m/7 ft 6 in; MM106 3 m/9 ft 9 in by 3.6 m/11 ft 9 in; and MM111 4 m/13 ft by 4.5 m/14 ft 6 in.

The smaller-growing plants produce fruit sooner, but the larger plants produce more fruit once they are established. Apple trees need another pollinating tree nearby in order to fruit well, so you may need to plant at least two of them, although there may be a pollinating tree in a neighbouring garden.

Malus x zumi var. calocarpa 'Golden Hornet'

CRAB APPLE

Situation	Full sun or dappled shade
Hardiness	Hardy (USDA zone 8)
Soil type	Moist, well drained
Height	10 m/32 ft 9 in
Spread	9 m/29 ft 6 in
Propagation	From grafts in winter
Flowering period	Spring
Fruiting period	Late summer to autumn

Crab apples have the same craggy outline as apple trees. Their fruits are extremely decorative and stay on the tree much longer than normal apples – unless, of course, you pick them and eat them. *Malus x zumi* var. calocarpa 'Golden Hornet' is included here for its lovely outline, although it offers other delights too. In spring, the fat pink buds become a profusion of blowsy white blossom, while in autumn the tree is smothered in bright yellow fruits. These light up your garden of an autumn dusk, hanging like Christmas baubles long after the leaves have dropped and well into winter.

These trees want the same conditions as apple trees – good, rich soil and full sun. However, since you don't need the fruits to ripen fully, they will tolerate a little light, dappled shade. Ideally, you shouldn't prune your crab apple much: they look better when they are allowed to grow naturally. If the centre of the plant becomes congested, it can lead to fungal problems from a lack of airflow. When that happens, it's best to prune. Do so in early summer, before the following year's flower buds have started to form, by cutting back any stems that cross in the middle to create an open, cup-shaped tree.

Nandina domestica

HEAVENLY BAMBOO

Situation	Sun or partial shade
Hardiness	Hardy (USDA zones 4–10)
Soil type	Rich, moist soil; likes acid soil but will tolerate others
Height	2 m/6 ft 6 in
Spread	1 m/3 ft 3 in
Propagation	Dig up and pot on runners
Flowering period	Summer

Nandina domestica is known as the heavenly bamboo. In fact, it isn't a true bamboo at all, but it fulfils a similar role in the evening garden by adding to the plant noises that help create a feeling of enclosure and distance from the outside world. Nandina leaves make a kind of papery rustling as the winds blows over it or as you run your hands through it (the papery texture makes it hard to resist touching it, too). Where it differs from most bamboos is in the fineness of its stems and its size. It grows to only around 2 m (6 ft 6 in) in height, making it useful for small gardens and suitable for a large pot.

Nandina's evergreen leaves change colour throughout the year, with new shoots a pinkish-coral, turning green, and then shades of red and orange in autumn. It holds onto those leaves all winter. Plumes of white flowers are produced in summer, and occasionally you may get a few red berries in winter too. Once planted and established, this is a plant that produces a great show yet needs very little care and attention: it is the perfect plant for a low-maintenance garden.

Phyllostachys nigra
BLACK BAMBOO

Situation	Full sun or partial shade
Hardiness	Hardy (USDA zone 8)
Soil type	Moist, well drained
Height	4 m/13 ft
Spread	3 m/9 ft 9 in
Propagation	Dig up, remove small chunks in spring, then replant
Flowering period	Non-flowering

As well as creating a dark, mysterious backdrop against which white and pale flowers can glow, *Phyllostachys nigra*, the black bamboo, has the added benefit of being a noisy plant. Admittedly, the noises are subtle – the swishing of the papery leaves and the knocking together of the woody stems – but subtle noises like these (the trickle of a fountain is another one) create a sense of atmosphere and help to block out extraneous sounds, like the noise of traffic or the hum of neighbours' voices. This is particularly important if you plan to use your garden for relaxation and quiet time, since it helps to focus your attention within.

P. nigra is a clumping bamboo, which means there is no danger of it running amok across your garden. It has fresh green leaves and glossy culms (the name given to the stems) of the deepest black. The culms emerge pale green in spring and turn black over the summer. To display them at their best and to emphasise their glossiness, thin out the oldest shoots and remove all the green growth to about one-third of the way up the stem. You can polish them, too, if you have time on your hands.

Prunus domestica
PLUM TREE

Situation	Full sun
Hardiness	Hardy (USDA zone 8)
Soil type	Moist, well drained
Height	Up to 9 m/29 ft 6 in, depending on rootstock
Spread	Up to 7 m/23 ft, depending on rootstock
Propagation	From cuttings in summer, but plants grown on their own rootstock can grow very large
Flowering period	Spring
Fruiting period	Late summer to autumn

Like apple trees, plum trees bear blossom in spring and fruits in summer. They are attractive trees and within a few years bring an air of maturity to a garden and will provide a craggy silhouette against which to plant night-scented plants.

Plum blossom appears fairly early in the year, so there is always the possibility that it will be hit by a late frost. To guard against this, it is important to plant your tree in a sunny, sheltered spot and to avoid any frost pockets – areas such as dips in the ground or the base of slopes where frost settles and lingers. Plant into rich soil that doesn't get waterlogged; plums particularly resent sitting in water.

Plum trees can grow large, so choose one grown on a dwarfing rootstock such as 'Pixy' or 'St Julien A'. They also have a bit of a reputation as biennial bearers, meaning that they produce lots of fruit one year and none the next. That's because the plant exhausts itself ripening its huge crop and doesn't manage to make the following year's flower buds. To prevent this from happening, thin out the fruits when they first form and again at the end of early summer, aiming for an eventual spacing of 5 cm/2 in between fruits. 'Victoria' is one of the most popular varieties of plum as it is self-fertile and delicious to boot. 'Oullin's Gage' is another good, self-fertile variety.

Prunus x subhirtella 'Autumnalis'

WINTER CHERRY

Situation	Full sun
Hardiness	Hardy (USDA zone 8)
Soil type	Moist, well drained
Height	8 m/26 ft
Spread	8 m/26 ft
Propagation	From cuttings in early summer
Flowering period	Late autumn to early spring

We think of ornamental cherries as producing a vast, hugely impressive flurry of blossom in spring, making previously naked trees look as though they are covered in candyfloss. *Prunus x subhirtella* 'Autumnalis' isn't like that. It is an ornamental cherry that blooms intermittently all winter long, only taking the occasional break when the weather is particularly chilly. So don't expect the same floral fireworks you would get from a spring-flowering cherry. This is a far more subtle creature, but it's a truly delightful plant and almost guarantees that you will have something pale and ghostly blooming away in your garden throughout winter. For a really pretty pale effect, grow some snowdrops around the base.

This tree works hard for most of the year. There's the winter blossom, obviously, then in spring the new growth is a pretty bronze colour. In autumn, the leaves turn orange and gold. Its only boring season is summer, but then there's so much else going on in the garden that you are unlikely to notice. It is a fairly compact tree and doesn't cast heavy shade, so both these qualities make it great for the smaller garden. Because of its open, light habit, you could easily grow a clematis or other small climber through its branches to make the tree earn its keep during summer, too.

Pyrus salicifolia 'Pendula'
WEEPING PEAR

Situation	Full sun
Hardiness	Hardy (USDA zone 8)
Soil type	Any
Height	5 m/16 ft 4 in
Spread	4 m/13 ft
Propagation	From grafts in winter
Flowering period	Spring

With its sweeping, pendulous stems, weeping pear provides a dramatic backdrop and its silvery leaves that glint in the moonlight make it a must for the night-time garden. It's a great tree for small gardens, reaching only 5 m/16 ft 4 in in height, but it does like to spread out, becoming almost as wide as it is tall. Its main charm, though, lies in those stems. They sweep down then curve upwards at the ends, as if they have changed their mind halfway. They bear white flowers in early summer.

This is a tough plant and will grow well in a range of soil conditions, including very dry and stony soil. It also takes seaside conditions in its stride and is drought-tolerant. But the one thing it won't tolerate is wet soil.

When it comes to pruning, you have two alternatives. Either plant it somewhere it can really spread and don't prune at all; just let it all hang out and develop that beautiful swooping structure. Alternatively, prune it each year into a huge lollipop shape, which looks better than it sounds. The result is a formal shape but with a lovely soft edge. Pruning the weeping pear like this means it can even be grown in smaller gardens or can be used as a recurring silvery accent plant throughout the garden. Prune in midsummer.

Sorbus cashmiriana
KASHMIR ROWAN

Situation	Full sun or partial shade
Hardiness	Hardy (USDA zone 8)
Soil type	Moist, well drained, slightly alkaline
Height	7 m/23 ft
Spread	6 m/19 ft 6 in
Propagation	Sow seed in autumn
Flowering period	Spring

The Kashmir rowan is a beautiful small tree that bears pink blossom in spring and berries in summer and autumn. While the common rowan's berries are bright red, those of *Sorbus cashmiriana* are large and pure white. They hang from fine, yellow-red stems in big, heavy bunches and show up, pure and pearly, in low light.

Although it eventually reaches quite a good size, this is a slow-growing tree and is a lovely choice for a small garden. Common rowans were traditionally planted outside front doors to ward away witches, and I see no reason why the same shouldn't go for the Kashmir rowan. In fact, I have one outside my own front door. It gradually spreads to become almost as wide as it is tall, and its leaves turn golden in autumn.

This tree does well in a range of soil conditions, although it seems to prefer a slightly alkaline soil, so avoid it if your soil is of the rhododendron-nurturing acid type. It is not as tough as the common rowan, so don't plant it in a frost pocket. Ideally, it needs sun and shelter from wind, although it will do pretty well in partial shade, too. Keep the soil moist and rich by mulching the roots with a thick layer of organic matter each year in autumn or spring.

Taxus baccata

YEW

Situation	Full sun to full shade
Hardiness	Hardy (USDA zone 8)
Soil type	Moist, well drained
Height	Up to 20 m/65 ft 6 in if left unpruned (usually grown as a hedge or topiary)
Spread	Up to 10 m/32 ft 9 in if left unpruned
Propagation	Sow seed in autumn or take cuttings in late summer
Flowering period	Cones in spring, berries in late summer

All the best floral displays need a good backdrop and there's none better than yew. It will give you a dense, dark, night-time backdrop for a pale, silvery planting.

Yew has small, fine-textured leaves of the deepest green and can be used a dense hedge or as fabulously tactile topiary. Both of these will set off those delicate, pale, night-time beauties to perfection. It is as though the yew is lending the garden the solidity it needs to counterbalance the fripperies. As an autumn and winter bonus, it produces bright red berries, which birds love.

Yew isn't the fastest-growing hedging plant, but neither is it as slow as many imagine. The density of its texture makes it worth waiting for. It is also incredibly long-lived: any yew hedge you plant could well last a couple of hundred years. So it's worth taking care when you plant it, making sure that the ground is well prepared. Dig out a trench and backfill it with garden compost mixed into the soil, then tread the soil down well. Use a line and pegs to lay out your hedge, and position the plants 45 cm/18 in apart. For a thicker hedge, plant a double row and stagger them.

Be warned that all parts of the plant are poisonous.

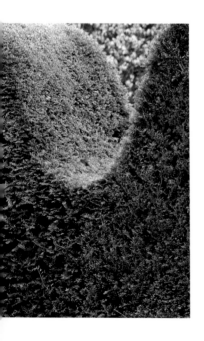

Trachycarpus fortunei
CHUSAN PALM, WINDMILL PALM

Situation	Full sun
Hardiness	Frost-hardy (USDA zone 10)
Soil type	Well drained
Height	10 m/32 ft 9 in
Spread	2.5 m/8 ft 2 in
Propagation	Sow seeds in spring or autumn in a heated propagator
Flowering period	Early summer

Trachycarpus is a plant that works beautifully in the night garden, creating a dramatic outline against the sky. Commonly known as the Chusan or windmill palm, it is one of the hardiest of the palms, so if you want to create a subtropical effect in a temperate garden, this is the one to try. It slowly forms a thick trunk covered in coarse, brown fibres that make it look hairy. At the top of the trunk it produces huge, palmate, fan-shaped leaves that stay on the plant year-round, providing valuable structure in winter. It grows slowly when young, but can grow as much as 30 cm/12 in a year once it is established. If you want to keep it small, grow it in a pot.

While trachycarpus likes a well-drained soil and will tolerate any soil except one that is permanently moist (it doesn't appreciate sitting in water over the winter), it will put on its best growth where there is adequate moisture. Once established, it will also tolerate drought.

A sunny or partially shaded spot is best, but the most important thing to remember when choosing a site is that it needs shelter from winds. The plant will grow fine but when the leaves are battered about, they start to look brown and tatty.

INDEX

patios 62
paving 50
heavenly bamboo 56, 194
hedgehogs 42
heliotrope 50, 90
heliotropium arborescens 50, 90
Helleborus niger 146
Hemerocallis citrina 65, 91
Hesperis matrionalis 43, 92–3
Himalayan birch 182
honeysuckle 27, 43, 55, 152
'Halliana' 102–3
hornbeam 184
Hydrangea arborescens 'Annabelle' 149

insects 20, 26
glow-worms 45
moths 43
Ipomoea alba 94
irrigation systems 50

Japanese wisteria 122–3
jasmine 26–7, 55, 96–7
Jasminum officinale 26–7, 55, 96–7
June berry 181

Kashmir rowan 201
Korean fir 180

lamb's ear 165
Laurus nobilis 191
lavender 150
Lavendula angustifolia 'Hidcote' 150
lawns 59, 62
lighting, using 31–5
contemplative gardens 56
for entertaining 65
family gardens 58–9
front gardens 49
in water features 38
lilies 26, 50
'Album' 98–9
day lilies 65, 91
trumpet lily 175
Lilium regale 'Album' 98–9
lily of the valley 137
Lobelia fulgens 37

Lonicera fragrantissima 152
Lonicera japonica 27, 43, 55
'Halliana' 102–3

Malus domestica 192
Malus x zumi var. calocarpa 'Golden Hornet' 193
marguerite 131
marvel of Peru 50, 106–7
Matthiola
M. bicornis 26, 50, 104
M. incana 104–5
Mexican orange blossom 65, 133
Mirabilis jalapa 50, 106–7
mock orange 154
moon-gazing party 68–9
moon-gazing ponds 37
moonflower 94
moonlighting 34–5
moths 43

Nandina domestica 56, 194
Nicotiana sylvestris 43, 108–9
night-blooming jessamine 82
night phlox 50, 124–5
night-scented hemerocallis 65
night-scented stock 26, 50, 104

Oenothera biennis 43, 65, 110–11
ornamental allium 128

Paeonia 'Claire de Lune' 153
paths 48–9
patios 62
paving 50
pergolas 26–7, 51, 55
Petunia 51
Tumbelina series 114–15
Philadelphus 'Beauclerk' 154
pinks 26
'Mrs Sinkins' 86–7
planning your garden 14, 19
colour 20–4
lighting 31–5, 49, 56, 58–9
organising space 47
scent 26–9, 49
style 48–59

TWILIGHT GARDEN 205

PICTURE CREDITS